THE AWARE ATHLETE

How the wild origins of our human nature and the new science of neuroplasticity are redefining fitness

SCOTT FORRESTER, GCFP

CONTENTS

SECTION 3: REDEFINING FITNESS

FOREWORD

Everyone has a different reason for delving into fitness, but fitness needs to be differentiated from exercise. Exercise maintains an organism. Fitness increases the potential of an organism, whether it be animal or human. My friend Scott's book, *The Aware Athlete*, takes you far beyond exercise and productivity to the process of developing your potential whether you are young or old, whether you consider yourself an athlete in the traditional sense or not.

Fitness requires a different level of mental tenacity than exercise does. Exercise takes substantially less willpower, time, energy output, and commitment than fitness does. Fitness is for those who see beyond the benefits of exercise and want more than its superficial effects. People focused on fitness become addicted to sculpting, both the invisible will and the mind-body. They want to experience more than just burning calories. They want to become masters of their domains.

While fitness and exercise are different, exercise is the first step on the road to physical fitness. With exercise, the muscles respond to new loads and new routines. The broader definition of fitness, though, encompasses the ability to adapt to all life's circumstances.

Exercise is the key to physical fitness; learning and adapting are the keys to life fitness. We must see the advantage of creating a lifestyle in which true health and wellness—the ability to find self-fulfillment and live our dreams—are priorities. Step two is committing to that lifestyle.

Fitness is always about movement. Physical fitness can be accomplished with many exercises and fitness systems. As a certified fitness trainer, I recognize two primary movements that increase fitness capacity: small and large. Most systems concentrate on one or the other. Pilates practitioners focus on slow, controlled, small movements. CrossFit® practitioners focus on large motor movements at high intensity. Both are difficult for different reasons. Both increase fitness and should, therefore, be done. Most athletes do one or the other. CrossFit® is now advocating that their athletes work on flexibility and accessory muscle groups. This is rarely done, however, and the deficiency is glaring. Barre, Pilates, and yoga folks could work on larger motor patterns with more intensity, but I doubt this is done often. Large and small muscle movements are yin and yang; both are needed.

Small, controlled, slow movements require purposeful effort. Like max static-hold movements, they require an enormous amount of concentration and focus. Large, high-intensity muscle movements require a different level of grit and willpower due to load on the skeletal frame. Both are necessary for whole-body fitness. In this book, Scott goes beyond physical fitness and the small movements of some exercise systems. He takes us to even finer, smaller, more differentiated movements that are characteristic of deep self-exploration.

But far beyond exercise, far beyond the common idea of what an athlete is, lies the concept of a person who strives to live their dreams, a person who pursues knowledge of the mind-body connection. An athlete is one who understands that mental movement and physical movement are the same.

It's becoming apparent in Western exercise physiology studies that there is no substitute for the mind-body connection. This is something that Eastern medicine has taught for thousands of years. To simply move a muscle without visualizing and actively engaging your mind to move it is just burning calories. It's just exercise. It's not well-rounded fitness. When we're engaged in a high-intensity workout, it is more difficult to do this. It can be done, but it takes a thorough background in meditation and active visualization to do this at high speed and under heavy load. Start slow. See every muscle moving in your head. Picture the muscle fibers. What are they doing? How are they moving? Why do you want them to move? What fitness goal are you trying to accomplish? Arnold Schwarzenegger was famous for using visualization in his workouts. He pictured exactly what he, as an athlete, expected to achieve by performing each repetition.

To engage the mind and body simultaneously takes time. It takes discipline and concerted effort. Human potential is found where mind meets body. This union is what the word "yoga" means. For thousands of years, Eastern medicine has spoken of this dialogue between mind and body using words such as *chi*, *ki*, and *prana*. For thousands of years in the East, physical movement was rarely spoken of as an isolated exercise. Emphasis was always placed on exercising the mind and body simultaneously. Martial artists and yoga practitioners have always taught that for an individual to be balanced, there cannot be one without the other.

In the West, we have a bit of catching up to do because we tend to have a dualistic view of the individual, that the body and brain are separate. We are beginning to understand the importance of this connection, but we don't have the *how* down yet.

The East offers us a lens through which we can more clearly see the mind-body connection. This lens is meditation. In the West, we are so accustomed to looking through an empirical lens that we cannot understand the value of experience. One day, I asked my meditation teacher of twenty-two years, "What is the nature of a master's mind?" She answered with an analogy. "Daughter, a master lives in the house. The rest of the people are merely looking at the blueprint of the house." Think on that. Contemplate that. It's the difference between telling someone about the color orange and seeing it. They are different levels of perception and awareness.

East is east, and west is west. But, there is a place where the two meet. Scott's book introduces readers to the work of Dr. Moshe Feldenkrais, a pioneer in the field of neuroplasticity. Feldenkrais was a scientist who introduced the Western world to a kind of mindfulness based on movement. He called his work Awareness Through Movement® (group lessons) and Functional Integration® (one-on-one work with a practitioner). Movement with awareness unites body and mind; it encourages you to be a whole person, not a collection of parts. Both are necessary. One without the other, movement without awareness, is a horse without a cart and vice versa. The two work in harmony.

There are thousands of teachers, authors, speakers, and personal growth mentors out there who claim they have the way to help you make the mind-body connection. This may or may not be true. What is true is that someone can only point the way. They cannot make the connection for you. They aren't the switchboard operator of your soul. It takes many hours of discipline to become the operator of your own mind. It takes as many hours per week of focusing the mind as it does to work your muscles. But, like moving your body, no one can do it for you. You must choose to pursue this worthy endeavor on your own. It is worth it. The way you move your body will not be the same. You will experience less effort, better results, less struggle, more fortitude, more options in life, improved inner flexibility, and greater ability to meet all life's challenges from within and without, and you will improve in both sport and life.

Like fitness, the benefits far outweigh the burdens of ardently pursuing this mind-body connection in athletics. What a wonderful thing to discover yourself more fully. We will understand this someday with science. We're already beginning to. It's said that most people only use 10 percent of their brain's potential. The real key to fitness is in the brain, not merely the muscles. The real key is in learning new skills, adapting to new challenges, inviting innovation into our lives. What potential for the athlete would there be if more than 10 percent were used? What astounding records would be broken? What unbelievable feats of fitness and movement would be shared with the world? The key is mindfulness. The door is you.

May you enjoy discovering a broader definition of fitness in the following pages. May your journey be powerful and your future bright.

Almine Barton, Licensed Acupuncturist, Certified Fitness Trainer, L1 CrossFit® Coach

ACKNOWLEDGMENTS

First, I would like to thank my wife of forty-five years, Lee Ann. Without her support through many years, and particularly the last two years of writing, *The Aware Athlete* would not have been possible. She is particularly responsible for taking and arranging pictures, checking many details, and being the first to read each iteration of this book (over and over).

Second, I would like to thank my editors: Stacy Ennis who got the editing process started and whose work went above and beyond what could have reasonably been expected, Robin Bethel whose astute observations provided a second round of substantive comments, and especially copy editor Cristen Iris who smoothed out the prose and asked many questions to make sure that she understood the intent of each passage and whose contributions helped us finish this project. Without the contributions of each, this book would not exist in its present form.

I thank friend, multi-sport athlete, coach, licensed acupuncturist, and spirited adventurer in life Almine Barton for being kind enough to write a foreword for the book. I am indebted to Sue Billington for telling her story of catastrophic injury and return to a life of doing what she loves. Sue, yours is the story of every athlete who suffers a profound setback and searches for answers. And I thank Stephanie Freeman for being an example of a true Aware Athlete, one who meets life's challenges, has developed profound strength, and never loses sight of serving others.

Last, I would like to thank all my good friends and colleagues in the Feldenkrais community and the Fulton Yoga Collective for their support of this project. And, of course, to all of you in the running and ultra-running communities who have supported me in this endeavor, thank you.

INTRODUCTION

This book is about you: your hopes and your dreams. It is about giving you the tools and understanding to experience your true potential. It is a book about a journey: your own journey of self-exploration and self-discovery. It is a journey of personal expansion. Along the way, you will find that you are capable of more than you thought, that nothing is impossible for you. For you are human and possess the most complex nervous system on the planet. You will discover the vast capacity for learning that the human species has and how science is exploding with new knowledge about the brain's capacity for change.

First, I hope you are not intimidated by the title of this book, *The Aware Athlete*. I use the word "athlete" in a broad sense. I am not referring only to professionally trained or highly paid athletes nor to those who participate in a particular sport.

The word "athlete" comes from the Greek word *athlein,* meaning "to contest for a prize." It is related to *athlos,* "a contest," and *athlon,* "a prize."[1]

---

1 athlete, Dictionary.com, *Dictionary.com Unabridged*, Random House, Inc. http://www.dictionary.com/browse/athlete?s=t

I use the word in a universal sense. I assume that most people are contesting for—seeking—some prize of personal value. I assume that most people want to live their dreams.

"Fitness" is defined as being fit or suited for something. For instance, the right tool for the job is fit for the job. Biological fitness is the ability to adapt, to fit the environment. I am, therefore, broadening the definition of fitness to be more than the idea of repetitions done, miles counted, and all things that can be measured. Instead, the content of this book reflects the original meaning of the word. When I refer to fitness in this book, unless otherwise noted, I am referring to your ability to adapt to all your inner and outer environments. I am referring to your ability to respond well to all circumstances and experiences in which you find yourself.

This book is for everyone interested in improving performance in sports or life, learning about and enjoying a new pursuit, moving with less joint pain, and experiencing longevity in doing the activities in life they love whether they are young or old. But, if you are looking for specific training programs, you will have to look elsewhere. I do not tell you exactly what to do. Rather, I attempt to lead you in the direction of self-exploration and discovery. I hope to encourage you to listen to your body and bring to light the awesome potential you have for living the life you want. Self-awareness and potential are cornerstones of the book.

This is not another book about trying harder and putting more effort into what you are doing in order to succeed. There is another element, one more truly human. It is the element of learning. No other animal has as deep an ability to learn, though plenty are stronger or faster than humans.

During my senior year in high school, I got involved with the track team. It was a manipulative thing. I wanted to change my schedule. I wasn't serious about track. If it didn't work out, I could always have dropped it and still have achieved my goal—having my schedule changed. Even though I didn't have any fitness for track, and a few weeks were not enough to develop it, I didn't quit. And it changed my life. I tried to walk on at a junior college and went through the first workout. I put in lots of effort, but the coach yelled at me for overstriding. This was years before running form was on the minds of most runners. Video analysis was not available, and I had no idea what he was talking about.

I continued to train on my own and decided that I would be more fit if I did two workouts per day. Not long after that, I suffered a painful stress fracture of my tibia. I wasn't a good runner when I was nineteen years old. I didn't know the difference between good running form and that which is not so good, nor did I have any understanding of running on a structural level. Putting in more effort did not help me achieve my potential. Will cannot make up for underdeveloped skill.

I have learned so much since then, and so will you as we explore together.

The material in *The Aware Athlete* is divided into three sections.

Section 1, The Wild Origins of Our Human Nature, raises the question of what it is to be human. In it, I describe what is unique about us and our species and how our biological heritage helps us define human fitness. Remember that fitness is defined by our ability to adapt to our environment.

Section 2, How Science Helps Us Understand Human Potential, explores the science of neuroplasticity and the related concept of mind-body unity, how the brain influences physical structures and our nervous system's ability to optimize movement and performance through mindfulness.

Section 3, Redefining Fitness, introduces a new fitness pyramid: a new concept about fitness and how to achieve it using personal awareness and the development of new skills.

At the end of each chapter, you will find one or more lessons. Most of these are movement lessons. Performing the movements and activities in each lesson will help you to experience the topics discussed in the chapter so they do not end up being only abstract ideas. Completing the lessons will allow you to experience mind-body unity. You may stop at the end of each chapter to do the lesson, or you may read through the whole book and then go back to review each chapter and do the associated lessons. Either way, your understanding of the material will not be complete without some exposure to personal exploration through movement. Fitness is always about movement.

But fitness is not only about movement. It is about what you can learn about *how* you move. It is about *your* learning process of sensing and feeling yourself as you do each movement that will help you to develop new skills and positive adaptations to your environment.

The intent of the movement lessons contained may be something you have not experienced before. The purpose of the lessons is not to exercise but to learn. I will give you instructions on how to do each lesson, but you should keep in mind that they are all to be done gently and at a slow-enough pace to allow your learning process to be smooth and thorough.

You may do the shorter lessons by reading through them and keeping the book handy for reference. The longer lessons have been divided into segments with steps to make them user-friendly.

Although it is not necessary, you may wish to record a lesson ahead of time using your computer or a voice recorder. If you decide to do this, please read the lesson slowly enough to allow time for you to organize yourself to do the movements, do a number of repetitions of each movement, and allow for rest periods as indicated in the lesson. Speak very slowly, and pause after sentences and indicated rest periods as you record.

• • •

My own journey led me to become a certified personal trainer; licensed physical therapist assistant; running form coach; and, finally, a Feldenkrais practitioner.

You'll often see the words "awareness" and "attention" in this book. I use many somatic movement lessons to help you develop thoughts and experience movement. I am deeply indebted to the pioneering work of Dr. Moshe Feldenkrais, who left an amazing legacy of over one thousand movement lessons and many books that inspired many of the lessons in this book. His lessons were developed through a lifetime of experimentation. Dr. Feldenkrais' work preceded and predicted the great breakthroughs in the areas of neuroplastic research that have occurred in the last two decades. The Feldenkrais Method® is still known as one of the most powerful tools available for achieving human potential.

There is much ground to cover, so let's begin our journey. We will redefine and broaden our definition of fitness and discover a new fitness pyramid. This will be a journey on which we will encounter much trial and error but little chance of failure if we embrace the process, if we esteem the journey more than the immediate goal.

SECTION 1

The Wild Origins of Our Human Nature:
What Is It to Be Human?

CHAPTER 1

Human Origins and the Environment

I am a human and I imagine. I imagine my origins. I imagine the Earth as a blank slate. "And the Earth was without form, and void; and darkness was upon the face of the deep."[2]

I imagine that I am the Earth: a vast, dark, and lonely ball of rock hurtling silently through space at great speed in a roughly circular orbit around a young star. I name my star Sun. I rotate around an axis allowing the light and heat of the Sun to spread over part of my surface while the other half remains in darkness. This process of rotation continues until eventually the Sun rises over my dark half. I call this cycle of light and dark day and night. The day is quite bright and the night extremely dark.

I see another great rock approaching. It is smaller than me. It seems to be heading straight toward me. It gets closer, and I see that it is not quite on a collision course. It approaches at a slight angle. I reach out to it with an invisible force of attraction and capture it. I name it Moon. And now, the Moon begins to arc around me in perfect balance and in perpetuity just as I orbit the Sun. I now have a companion, a sister. I

---

2 Genesis 1:2. Bible, King James Version.

am not so alone. I cling to the Moon as a friend. In return, the Moon, standing as a beacon in space, reflects some of the Sun's light onto my dark side and lights the night.

I call my vast rock a planet. Much of my planet's surface is covered by water. I feel immense lengths of time pass as I orbit my sun, repeating the cycles of day and night. Most of the face of my planet is covered by water but not all. There is bare rock and land standing above the watery expanses. Time passes in enormous eternal waves. As time passes, things change. I feel that I am organizing myself in new ways. My core is hot and, from time to time, I belch hot gases. I hold onto a thin layer of gas above my surface, a layer of gas that extends miles above. Change continues. I am amazed at what I am capable of now.

This process of change occurs at an ever-increasing rate. It is complicated. I am now a complex environment. Chemical reactions occur. I am home to ever more minute and interesting phenomena. As I orbit the Sun, I see self-sustaining processes occur within my sphere. I organize myself to support these processes, and some of them I call "life." Life can use the environment that I supply to maintain itself, to grow, and to reproduce. How interesting; I am now not alone on my planet. I have friends in the sky, and I am home to those who choose to live with me. Soon life is teeming on my surface. I am the Earth. I am unique. I have a purpose, and my story is a story of life and death. There is so much life now.

I imagine myself as a single-celled organism, a bacterium. I multiply quickly. Perhaps I will inherit the Earth. But sometimes I find myself in an environment that is too hot or too cold. I have not adapted. I feel my functions slowing, my life ebbing. I cannot survive. I die, but in dying am reborn, replaced by others. I die and am consumed by other organisms, but the process of living goes on. I am replaced by more successful organisms. I am learning that living involves the struggle to maintain all life's components in balance. I must adapt. I must change to meet new challenges.

I imagine myself as many cells making up one organism. I evolve and become more complex. I imagine the possibilities of multicellular life-forms. I see many complex animals that adapt to fill the seas, the depths, the skies, and every niche on land. My soil blossoms with greenery. This is beautiful but vicious. Life has names: plants, animals. To survive, they must consume others for energy. They must also escape being consumed. To adapt, I see myself becoming larger, then larger still. I envision myself as a dinosaur, the most massive with the most brute strength of any animal to live on land. I am unassailable, unbeatable. I eat what I want, and I survive. I thrive. I do inherit the Earth for many millions of years. Strength, size, ferocity, these are ingredients of my success. I am challenged by none. None like me has arisen before, and none has ruled the Earth this long.

But today I see a sight in the sky, a grand light burning through the atmosphere, a huge rock from space that, in an instant, explodes with a force the magnitude of which obliterates all that is close to its place of impact in a massive fireball. It sends debris far into the sky. The force of the impact is unimaginable, generated by a rock 6 miles wide and traveling perhaps 50,000 miles per hour. The impact crater is over 100 miles wide. Dust and debris travel around the globe. Day is turned into night. The blackness below the dark clouds creates a winter that lasts years. The Earth is rattled and shaken; volcanoes become more active. But I have already died, and with me has gone three quarters of life on Earth. My size and strength could not save me. As a dinosaur, my reign was long, but I have perished.

Eventually, the clouds settle. The Sun's rays reach the surface again. But the great experiment in size and strength is over. Some species have survived. New eras follow.

Complex animal life continues. Other animals arise. Instead of larger size and more brute strength and muscular power, a new trend starts. I am now a human, an animal of relatively little size, speed, or strength but possessing the most highly developed nervous system on the planet. I, as the human animal, must also survive. How humans manage to survive, adapt, and prosper, will be the story I now tell.

It is a human characteristic to contemplate our beginnings. It is said that all cultures have origin stories. The stories typically move from blank slate—from nothing—until, step by step, they arrive at mankind. Life requires two things. First, it requires an environment. The environment, in its strictest sense, is the Earth. It is air, sunlight, water, food, and gravity. Without the environment, there would be no humanity.

Second, life requires interaction with our planet: with nature, with other life. It is this necessary interaction that moves life from simple to complex, from single cells to multicellular to societal life. All this increased complexity results in more options for survival; adaptation; prosperity; and, ultimately, self-consciousness and enjoyment.

From the human standpoint, the sum of all our interactions is the environment. We can, therefore, broaden the definition of the environment. Our environment includes our inner environment and all the interactions of our individual cells and systems as well as our thoughts, feelings, backgrounds, and attitudes. Our outer environment includes the physical qualities of our surroundings and geographic location and our ability to move in them: gravity, our interactions with other people, social structures, workplaces, family, background, individual stresses, etcetera. In the broadest sense, the environment is any situation in which we find ourselves. Particularly, it is the interactions we have when we want to or attempt to do something we desire to do. The process of living requires constant adaptation. Successful adaptation is the goal. This is fitness.

. . .

I recently talked to someone who had developed tenderness along the shins (shin splints) from running on a treadmill. They described how they ran through the pain and that it got worse as a result. What is not widely known is that you can run through many running injuries, but only *if* you know how to make a successful change: a successful adaptation or improvement to *how* you are doing what you are doing. Adaptation is the key to improvement, interacting with your environment and learning its requirements. It will not come about by ignoring your interactions with the environment, as in running through the pain.

Another point that can be made about fitness and adaptation is that fitness is not about strength, size, power, or even physical toughness. Remember the dinosaurs, the largest and strongest creatures ever? They died off abruptly. Fitness is about the ability to respond favorably to a changing environment.

All life and all higher animals must adapt in the environment in order to survive. Indeed, man is an animal. I will soon take up the subject of the difference between man and other higher animals. But before I do, consider what you have in common—your kinship—with other mammals. It is one thing to say we are animals, another to feel it. As you consider your similarities to other animals, your relationship to the environment, your need to maintain your body temperature, and the fragility of your life, I will tell you a story.

It was September in the high mountains of the Wind River Range in western Wyoming. I had packed light but carried enough gear to survive whatever conditions I might encounter. Within the limits of the gear I had chosen, I had packed for survival, not for comfort. I was now at those limits as the weather changed. I had had good shelter from the rain earlier in the trip. I strung my rain poncho over myself and tied it to trees. With the sides open, the shelter was well ventilated. But it got much colder than it had been a few days before, and I worried about protection from the wind. I made the mistake of trying to shelter behind huge boulders. They did not protect me from the breeze, and, to make matters worse, they were on slightly higher and uneven ground. I kept sliding downhill during the night and had to keep moving back up the slope. It was the worst campsite of my trip.

As soon as darkness descended, I began hearing noises. I turned on my headlamp, but the evening mist reflected light back at me. I could only see the distance of a few feet in front of me. I snuggled next to the giant rocks, turned off my light, and tried to go to sleep. I turned the headlamp on again briefly and noted a spider crawling into a crack in the rocks. I marveled that it could survive the cold of that night. I wondered how it could maintain its body temperature. I shared my bed with the spider. I was no different than it at the moment. We were both exposed animals trying to survive a cold night.

I didn't sleep much. The night got colder as time went on. I got up in the middle of the night, then tucked myself back into my 1-pound sleeping bag. It was big enough to cover my large frame well and made with high-loft down but was very thin. I sat up part of the night. I began to shiver, hungry from a week spent in the mountains. I was tired but wanted to monitor my shivering. Shivering is the body's way of staying warm; it is also an early sign of hypothermia. Nothing progressed beyond shivering though. I tucked my entire head into my bag and closed the hood, leaving only a small hole that allowed me to fill my bag with the warm air I exhaled. I occasionally opened the bag a bit so it wouldn't accumulate too much moisture from my breath, then I closed the bag again.

Eventually, the sky lightened, and I packed up. My shoes were hard with icy frost. I put on my stiff shoes that matched my cold, stiff body and began to take slow steps toward the trail.

It is one thing to know you have a lot in common with the animal kingdom. It is another to feel yourself just as vulnerable and exposed as they are, to share your bed with a spider, and after a few days to feel that you yourself are an animal. In fact, we can envy the other animals' uncanny ability to survive.

Have you ever experienced a long, cold night in which you were tired and out of food? If you have, you know that there is no doubt that humans are animals, mammals. Like other mammals, we struggle to survive.

. . .

We might not say that man is in every situation more intelligent than other animals. Nonhuman animals sometimes put humans to shame with their ability to adapt to the environment and live and thrive in conditions we cannot. They have great intelligence. They often have great memories and can perform mental feats humans can't. Some of them make tools and use strategies. All animals, humans included, are shaped by their histories, their interactions with the environment. We could say that life is defined as being the sum of all our interactions with the environment.

So, before we start the next chapter, I invite you to think about what the difference between humans and other animals is. What special characteristic do you think separates us from all other animals? Doing the movement lessons at the end of this chapter will give you some clues.

CHAPTER 1 LESSON:
THE PURPOSE OF POSTURE

Everything—including our safety, health, and progress in life—depends on our interaction with the environment. Even our ideas about good posture originate and are conditioned by our interaction with it. This lesson focuses on this often-overlooked aspect of our daily interactions with the world around us.

Like all lessons in this book, remember to do the movements gently. You will be able to observe more and get more benefit from the lesson this way. Remember, the object is to learn to move better—to interact more with the environment—not to just do movements. Go slowly. Pay attention to *how* you do what you do.

· · ·

Take your time: Allow 20–30 minutes to experience and experiment with this lesson.

It will be helpful to have a chair nearby.

1. Stand and notice what your standing is like. What is your general sense of your standing, your sense of ease, and where do you look when you are standing naturally? Where is the horizon? Notice and observe, then walk around for a few moments.

2. Come back to standing on the spot where you started and then imagine you are in an environment where the grass grows tall and there are predators all around. You are standing in a clear spot. How do you need to stand? Stand in a way that maximizes

the distance you can see. Can you see over the tall grass and obstacles? Perhaps you can see to the horizon. Can you organize yourself so you can look quickly to the left and right? Can you turn quickly to look behind you? Are you standing in a way that allows you to quickly move in any direction: up, down, right, left, forward, or backward? Can you see how awareness in the environment influences posture?

3. Sit in the chair. Notice how you sit. How do you do it? Are your feet on the floor? Can you feel your sitting bones on the chair? How far can you see? Now imagine yourself sitting on a rock. Can you arrange yourself to see over obstacles and be prepared to move in any direction at any time?

4. In this setting, we can define good posture as the ability to be situationally aware and see and move in any direction for the purpose of survival. How are you sitting after putting yourself in a context in which situational awareness means survival, one in which being able to see over obstacles is a prime need? What are the differences in the way you stand or sit now? Can you imagine a threat behind you, a need to get to your feet? Can you see how your movement is shaped by the environment? Are you finding that you can move more quickly and lightly than you thought possible?

Congratulations. You have just done something no other animal can do. You have—through directed attention and self-awareness—reflected on your movement by noticing and integrating an action that includes all parts of yourself. You have improved your movement. You can do this because you are part of a species we call human.

CHAPTER 2

Animal Magic versus Human Magic

I am a human, and I believe in magic. I have seen great powers at work in the night sky. I see the Moon, and I observe. I watch carefully and see the Moon repeat its cycle in the sky. The Moon and tides correspond. How can this be? This is the greatest of magic. I look carefully for a very long time. My sight is keen. I imagine mountains on the Moon. I imagine valleys. I see symbols. I marvel at how the Moon's appearance changes in size and color. Is the Moon another world? If the Moon is a world of its own, what is the mighty Sun, the giver of light, warmth, and life?

I know that there are unseen forces, forces that are more than natural, more than the eye can see. They are forces I cannot fully understand, and yet I know them each day. How can the Moon reach out with invisible fingers and touch the Earth, touch the waters? How can the two be one?

I see the Sun return without fail each day in relentless succession: the epitome of trustworthiness and power. What unseen power causes this to happen? The Sun has a special relationship with the Earth, a covenant that cannot be broken.

I see a woman whose belly is swollen with child. I see the child grow larger, and I behold the day of its birth. This is a great mystery. Does this new life come from nowhere? How can it come forth and be formed inside a woman? Does this new life come from another world, a place unseen? I see the relationship, a man with a woman. We are separate, yet we are related to each other, to the life to come, to the Earth, the Moon, the Sun. All things are related.

I think of myself. I observe my thoughts. I watch, and I see a universe of thought, feeling, possibility, relationship. Where is my place? I of all the animals contemplate these things. I alone take this in and rearrange it. I alone possess the ability to remake my world. It is the nature of man to plumb the depths of the infinite, the unknown, and to seek to know more, to be more.

All animals have a unique way of coping with and enjoying the environment. This chapter compares other animals' unique survival strategies to the human animal's unique ability to adapt and survive. Notice that humans are the ones to do the musings in the dialog above, the only ones who spend so much time thinking about the unseen and unknown. The difference between humans and other animals is not just intelligence, as you will see, but a special kind of intelligence.

I have used the word "magic" in the title of this chapter. Humans and other animals exhibit a special kind of magic. Let's examine and compare each kind of magic.

Magic is

1. having or apparently having supernatural powers;

2. very effective in producing results, especially desired ones;

3. wonderful; exciting.

I use the word "magic" as defined by numbers two and three: very effective and indeed wonderful. The examples I will give are more than mere animal studies. They reveal the creative and wonderful interactions of each species with their environments. I find these examples fascinating. It is up to you to decide whether you wish to add the first definition to this discussion.

Animal magic is the special adaptive strategies of each species. Human magic, which I will discuss after animal magic, refers to the unique human adaptive strategy.

Animal life appears mysterious and powerful. The arctic tern migrates over longer distances than any other bird. It is said to fly over 1.5 million miles in a lifetime. Imagine ranging over the whole globe each year from the arctic regions to the Antarctic, timing your migration to find food and a survivable climate year-round, seeing more of the world than any other animal, and, because of the timing of the yearly journey, spending more time in daylight than any other animal. The birds split their path as they fly south. Half of them follow more or less the North and South American continents. Half of them journey south on the other side of the Atlantic Ocean, following more or less the African continent. When the journey is done, they meet off the Antarctic continent. How do they do this? How do they get the timing and location right? What marvelous adaptations do they have for long-distance flight? On their return journey, they take a more direct route and sometimes cover up to 300 miles per day. It is an effective, mysterious dance with the environment.[3]

3 Powell, Hugh, Editor, "Arctic Tern," The Cornell Lab of Ornithology, Cornell University, Ithica, New York. 2015, https://www.allaboutbirds.org/guide/Arctic_Tern/id

Polar bears have adapted to extreme cold environments. They grow thick layers of fur and subcutaneous fat. They can swim in icy waters and sleep on frozen tundra. Black and grizzly bears can slow their metabolisms and wait out the cold winters in their dens until spring arrives and it is again time to gorge themselves. Dogs have an incredible sense of smell. The arctic fox can smell food under the snow and frozen ground. Antelope are the fastest animals on land over a distance. They can reach speeds of 60 mph and maintain speeds of 30–40 mph for 20 miles.[4] Ants work together as a society and have a form of unspoken communication. How do they do it?

Some insects can increase production of glycerol in the winter and use it as a kind of antifreeze to prevent cell damage at sub-freezing temperatures. Like bears, insects lower their metabolisms when the weather is cold.

All these adaptations beg questions. They also inspire us to consider what is possible. These behaviors evoke a sense of awe. What kind of intelligence allows the creatures of the Earth to do these unimaginable things?

. . .

HOW INTELLIGENT ARE ANIMALS?

One study shows that when chimps briefly viewed numbers on a computer screen, they were able to recall the positions of the numbers better than college student volunteers. Numbers were displayed briefly on the computer screens and then replaced by blank squares.

---

4 Conservation Institute.org, "10 Fastest Animals on Earth, #5 Pronghorn Antelope," Conservation Institute (2017), http://www.conservationinstitute. org/10-fastest-animals-on-Earth/

The trial was done using three different time intervals. The chimps were able to remember the position of the numbers at the shortest time intervals. The conclusion was that the chimps were using a kind of photographic memory. This shows that chimps and other animals can often outperform humans when performing certain tasks both mental and physical.[5] Many animals do things that are far beyond our abilities.

In *Ape Genius*, primates are shown to be able to cooperate with each other to obtain food.[6] They learn new behaviors by watching each other and humans. Some primates have learned up to three thousand words and recognize other symbols. They live in groups and so can pass on knowledge and skill to the next generation as the young observe the actions of the adults. They even make tools such as primitive spears for hunting.

In one experiment, a clear plastic tube was placed inside a chimp's cage. Clearly visible inside the tube was one peanut in a shell. The chimp tried to reach into the tube to get the peanut, but its hands would not fit. The chimp sat looking at the puzzle for 10 minutes. Suddenly, it got up and went to a water container, filled its mouth, went back to the apparatus, and spit the water into the container. It repeated this process three times until the peanut floated to the top of the tube where the chimp could reach it.[7] Would you have thought of that?

All these animal abilities demonstrate great intelligence and are examples of the fundamental definition of fitness. Fitness is the

---

5 Main, Douglas, "Chimps Have Better Short-term Memories Than Humans" (February 16, 2013), http://www.livescience.com/27199-chimps-smarter-memory-humans.html

6 "Ape Genius," NOVA (PBS Documentary, posted by Science Output August 15, 2015), https://www.youtube.com/watch?v=ElayXhaaLD0

7 "Ape Genius," NOVA (PBS Documentary, posted by Science Output August 15, 2015), https://www.youtube.com/watch?v=ElayXhaaLD0

ability to adapt to the environment. Yet as we will see, there is an essential human quality that allows adaptation—evolution if you will—to take place at much faster speeds in human populations.

• • •

HUMAN MAGIC

All the animals I have mentioned have biologically effective survival strategies. So, biologically, what distinguishes us as human and what is the unique human survival advantage? What is human biological magic? I am a human, but what is that? I am intelligent, but so are all the higher animals that surround me. I am conscious, but that is not unique to me. As a human, I know my way around my environment, but so do other animals. I hunt. I reproduce. I remember. I cooperate with members of my family and tribe. I communicate. But this is not special. Animals make many distinctions. Dogs know when they are biting hard or just nipping. They know what the bark or growl of another dog means. They recognize many sounds and words and read body language. They know the road home.

Here is the difference between mankind and other animals: no other animal is able to think in abstract terms. Feldenkrais puts it succinctly: "There is no doubt that abstraction remains the exclusive province of man, the harmonic theory in music, space geometry, the theory of groups, or probability are unimaginable outside of man's own mind."[8] This difference is what allows humans to adapt to the environment in more flexible ways than any other animal.

8 Feldenkrais, Moshe; *Awareness Through Movement*; Harper One (1972) 40

Other animal species occupy their own niche on the planet, having made very specific and effective adaptations. Humans occupy almost every niche on the planet from the arctic to the tropics and from the highest altitudes to the lowest. Some humans even live in nuclear-powered submarines for weeks or months at a time below the surface of the sea.

We do this by modifying our environment to suit our needs. For better or worse, humans are currently the dominant species on the planet. How did this happen? By process. A process of (1) abstract thinking and (2) preserving and sharing what we've learned. Humans have managed to learn to store and retrieve information through oral tradition and externally on stone, parchment, by engraving metal, writing in books, and storing electronically. They pass the information to others by extensive communication and schooling, so the bank of knowledge on the planet continues to grow with each generation. Human survival has always been a social, connected endeavor. Otherwise, no individual human would have survived.

Society is a critical outgrowth of learning and knowledge preservation. Likewise, teamwork and shared labor are human characteristics arising from the extremely complex human brain and nervous system. The human experience involves intense interaction with the environment, including all its social and physical aspects.

All humans have outer and inner environments. The knowledge base of the human species is increasing and involves the outer environment. Mankind has learned to make energy-efficient housing that is warm in the winter and cool in the summer. We make many styles and applications of clothing to suit the conditions and live in cities that are safe from most predators (except other humans). Survival is hard, and humanity seizes opportunities to make it easier:

learning to sow and cultivate crops so food is close by, domesticate animals and harness their power and energy to do work and raise them for meat. We went from surviving more easily to thriving in a perilous world by building more permanent settlements. Continuing to learn, we began to specialize, utilizing the power of the individual while forming more complex societies. We improved the powerful tools of speech and language and use new knowledge to our advantage.

Turning attention to the inner environment, we study medicine to rid ourselves of diseases. We have other disciplines too: psychology, anatomy, physiology, philosophy, physics, biology, chemistry, and religion. Seeking is endless; so is curiosity.

The ability to think in abstract terms and learn more and more deeply is what gives humans their primary biological and adaptive advantage. The ability to learn actually stands above the evolutionary process. Humans can adapt more quickly than the evolutionary process usually allows. Putting on a warm coat is a quicker adaptation than waiting for nature to provide thicker or thinner fur as climate changes. We adapt to potentially life-threatening environmental influences like heat and cold in many ways.

• • •

WHAT IS ABSTRACT THINKING?

Do humans have a unique and special way of thinking, a kind of thinking that actually slows down our mental processes? We humans have the ability to insert a gap—a time space—between thinking and acting. That space between thinking and acting is the realm of the abstract, the reflective. It gives us the ability to separate from ourselves and our environment, to conceptualize, to wonder, to imagine.

But, there is a special kind of abstract knowing that I have not yet mentioned. There is a knowing called *awareness*. It includes self-knowing, or self-awareness, and this knowledge has been sought after for many centuries. Self-knowledge is the key to thriving in life, to doing what you really want.

Awareness can be defined as the ability to observe oneself—or more concretely—to focus attention on the matter at hand for the purpose of improving action.

Using abstract thinking, humans can cut a situation into its parts and reorganize them into new patterns that result in the learning of new skills. With awareness—or mindfulness—comes the ability to continually learn or experience mind-body improvement through-out life. All this is possible thanks to the realm of abstract thought.

The lesson at the end of this chapter demonstrates how this works. In it, you will use mindfulness to observe your movement and will develop your ability to shift attention to parts of yourself and observe how they affect the whole of yourself. By placing the parts into different contexts and observing the results as a whole, you may be able to observe your habits. And by observing, you will introduce yourself to the process of creating new, more efficient patterns of standing, walking, and moving in the world. You will experience through movement the use of awareness and abstract thinking in creating new, more skillful self-usage. You will find that as you perform and revisit this lesson in the future that there is no end to what you can learn and the improvement you can make. This cutting of a whole into parts and rearranging them to form a new creation, a new whole, is an ability that opens up new possibilities for the human species to do things that no other creature on Earth can do.

Another word that helps to define abstract thought is "imagination." Imagination is the ability to take an image and insert it into a new context, thus creating something new from something already known. They say that the sky is the limit, yet mankind has been to the Moon. And the imagination knows no bounds.

The ability to think in this abstract way opens up new possibilities for our species, and for us as individuals there is astounding potential. In the next chapter, I tell the story of how little-known athlete Billy Mills won an Olympic gold medal by using his imagination to create a new idea of what was possible for him. This is abstract thought: taking an existing idea—the winning of a race—and putting it into a different context, in this case a personal context. This essentially human idea of thinking in abstract terms allows you to reshape your personal world as well as contribute to shaping the world at large.

CHAPTER 2 LESSON:

DIFFERENTIATE AND INTEGRATE MOVEMENT

This lesson is a good example of abstract thinking and the conscious, organized, methodical process that humans can enter but animals cannot.

• • •

Take your time: Allow 30 minutes to complete this lesson and take stock of the results.

1. Please stand. Get a sense of your standing. How effortless is your standing? Where do you sense tension or relative ease? Does your standing feel natural to you? Sense the amount of weight on each foot. Is it equal or does one side feel heavier than the other?

2. Shift a little of your weight to the outsides of your feet. Shift just enough weight to be able to notice the difference this shift makes to your standing. To improve, you must be able to sense differences. What happens in your ankles when you do this? Can you sense the muscles in your lower legs? How are they involved? Do you notice a change in your knees, hips, your pelvis, and your low back?

3. Walk around like this for a minute. Was this different from the way you normally walk? Take a brief rest while standing in this new way.

4. Come back to standing in your normal way. Can you bring more weight to the insides of your feet? Pay attention to what this does

in the arches of your feet and in your knees. What is the effect on your overall posture? Walk around like this for a minute.

5. Take a brief rest.

6. Come back to standing normally, then take a little more of your weight into your heels. This time, pay even more attention to your overall pattern of standing. What is different when you take more weight into your heels? Notice what happens in your feet, knees, thighs, pelvis, and spine. Also notice what effect this has on your balance. How does your balance change when you stand with more weight on your heels? Do you feel any activation of your lower leg muscles, back muscles, and/or thighs that counteracts the change in balance? If your balance changes by shifting weight into your heels, does your breathing change? Do you sense any change in tone in your throat, jaw, face, and chest?

7. Walk around this way for a minute.

8. Rest briefly.

9. Come back to standing. Can you shift more of your weight into the balls of your feet? What effect does this have? Walk around this way for a minute.

10. Come back to standing normally. Notice any changes in the way you stand. Did one of these patterns seem closer to the way you normally stand and walk? Perhaps you have discovered something about your habits. Have you sensed or discovered anything new? Do your standing and walking feel any different?

. . .

You have just taken the already-known idea of standing and shifting your weight and *noticed* things about your standing, your habits. By doing this, you have created more personal awareness. By doing so, you may have created a new way of standing and walking. In this lesson, you focused on the parts of the feet, then shifted your attention to other parts and to the whole.

By shifting your attention back and forth, you began to discover how to integrate a change in a part with the whole. You learned to make an entirely different pattern. By observing your sense of comfort, your breathing, your overall effort in standing, you may have found that you like some of these patterns more than others. When you need to change movement patterns, when you have sustained an injury, for example, or when you want more movement options for different situations, you can use the process of sensing the part, then sensing the whole, shifting back and forth between the two to integrate a new pattern. This kind of practice will promote more awareness about what you are doing as you participate in your favorite activities.

The sensing you did in this lesson is transferable to many situations. And in this lesson, you engaged in a uniquely human ability: the ability to observe, sense, and reorganize yourself.

CHAPTER 3

Dreams Realized: The Integration of Imagination and Action

I often see the mighty lion kill its prey. The lion hunts prey both larger and smaller than itself. The lion has killed many antelope. I watch, and this time I see an antelope use its speed to evade the lion. Now I know that the lion does not always win. I see the lion attack a buffalo. The lion jumps on the buffalo's back and holds on with its claws, attempting to bite into its prey's neck. But the buffalo's hide is tough, and the buffalo has time to toss the lion off its back. In an instant, the buffalo swings its head. Its horn sinks deep into the lion's side under its front leg. The wounded lion has had enough and limps away into the brush. The buffalo has won this time. I see all this and wonder. The buffalo used horns to fend off the lion's attack. I find a skull with a set of horns; they are from an animal with straight horns, not the curved horns of the buffalo. I mount the horns on a stout stick. I show this device to others, and we make more of them. Now we have something with which to fend off a lion.

To imagine is to use the abstract mind to place an image in a new context. The image of the horn has been placed in a new context as an image of a tool for defense that a human could use. This creates new, bold, and risky but sustainable possibilities and is a skillful adaptation to the environment. The beginning of imagining a new tool directs us toward continual refinement until at last there is no doubt that we have transcended our original place in the environment. The person or persons who developed better spearheads benefited themselves, their group or society, and even the next generations.

Imagination can direct us toward new possibilities constructed by rearranging things we observe. We call this potential as demonstrated in the following quote from Napoleon Hill: "Whatever the mind of man can conceive and believe, it can achieve."[9] Our potential is like a vast, unexplored continent.

Utilizing imagination to form new patterns of action in line with our dreams is how we live life to its fullest. This is what takes humans to the skies and makes voyages to the Moon and exploration of other planets possible. Developing imagination related to action allows us to improve movement, achieve goals, and change habits. Using this power, we can create new realities for ourselves.

In 1964, Native-American athlete Billy Mills won the gold medal in the Olympic 10,000-meter run, besting world-record holder Ron Clark. Mills came up from third place in the final meters with an astounding sprint that looked almost impossible. Little regarded before the race, Mills had stunned the world. How did he do it? According to Mills, "The subconscious mind doesn't know the difference between reality and imagination.[10]"

9 Hill, Napoleon; *Think and Grow Rich*; Napoleon Hill Foundation, Wise, Virginia (1937)

10 Mills, Billy, "How to Visualize," One Vision Board (March 21, 2012), https://www.youtube.com/watch?v=Fx1GBrQEzjw

There is an inner world and an outer world, and the two must be integrated. Mills learned not one new motor skill and not one new psychological ability but many. He put them all together during several years of practice and turned imagination into reality. Mills was able to form habits that allowed him to face the greatest competitors in the world and the high pressure of the last 60 yards of the race, including the unexpected shove he received on the last lap. His success was not only imagined but sustained in a real-life situation because he'd developed mental toughness, something Cathy McMahon talks about in *Survival Mindset*: "Our ability to confront and endure misfortune will center on our ability to acquire habits of mind that will pull us through."[11]

Mills had spent four years training daily for the 10,000-meter race and had visualized his winning outcome dozens of times each day. Mills combined systematic training with a systematic process of believing that he could compete with the best in the world. With just meters to go on the final lap, he began to say to himself, I've won, I've won, even though he was in third place. Within seconds, the thing he had visualized for years became reality as he stayed loose and passed Ron Clark for the win. At that time, his was the fastest time ever run by an American.

Mills' story shows us we can use our physical imagination not only to conceive of what we want but to achieve it. Physical imagination is a powerful tool in the development of better movement and better habits. However, this story is really a synopsis, a summary of what happened. As such, it is an oversimplification. In truth, each journey toward a long-term goal contains many individual

11 McMahon, Kathy, "The Survival Mindset," Resilience, Post Carbon Institute 800 SW Washington Ave. Suite 5, Corvallis, OR 97333 USA (March 2010), http://www. resilience.org/stories/2010-03-15/survival-mindset

learning experiences. In Mills' case, he broke each challenge into pieces and then reassembled them into new, useful skills: the skill of sprinting, sprinting when tired, staying loose, developing a long-distance stride and the efficient use of energy, developing confidence in his ability to compete and a winning race strategy, training in a way that promoted his optimal pace yet didn't tear his body down, and training that improved or maintained his running form over time. Many pieces were put together, all built on the foundation of human awareness and the ever-adaptable human nervous system.

As you can see, Mills employed not only visualization of the desired outcome of winning a gold medal in the Olympics, he also refined many sensory-motor skills. In order to achieve our goals—to live our dreams—we must do both. Now consider how the physical accomplishment of winning the gold medal changed Mills' self-image.[12]

Our thoughts become our realities. We can align our thoughts with our dreams. We can align our movement with our thoughts—our feelings. Our ability to adapt inwardly to outward challenges is a key to unlocking our potential and our achievement. Everything starts with strong individuals, but it doesn't end there. Mills' life was changed after winning that gold medal. He has gone on to help and inspire countless others and cofounded the nonprofit Running Strong that supports Native-American children.

Remember the lion on the savanna? Fear is a primal emotion for all of us. Our challenges are rooted in our fears. Everyone has the fear instinct, and everyone has moments of fear. Courage is doing

---

12 Mills, Billy, "How to Visualize," One Vision Board (March 21, 2012), https://www. youtube.com/watch?v=Fx1GBrQEzjw

what must be done even though you fear doing it. It's important to remember that thinking that does not lead to better action is not real thinking but mere *cerebration,* as Feldenkrais referred to it. Thinking and acting are parts of the same process. Michael Port, in his book *Steal the Show,* speaks of performance saying, "The acting as if technique gives you the opportunity to become the thing you're imagining yourself to be. You act *as if* you are in charge, you act *as if* you are calm, and you act *as if* you look forward to speaking to large groups. And slowly, those things become more and more true. And your performances become more and more natural."[13]

Can you see how an actor needs to integrate thoughts, emotions, and physical actions to master their craft? Can you see how everyone needs to do the same? Can you see how acting *as if* is a practical part of the process of imagining and visualizing? In a sense, you are not acting *as if*; you are actually, in this moment, being the person you want to be. The point is that you are taking action; you are acting. For an actor to desire a role is one thing. For him or her to learn to act *as if,* to take action to immerse himself or herself in the craft, is another. For primitive man to imagine a spear is one thing. To have the courage to use it is another. For Billy Mills to imagine victory was one thing. To act out the entire focused training process was another.

Imagination without action is nothing, but imagination plus action is the key to new realities, new dreams.

• • •

13 Port, Michael, *Steal the Show,* Houghton Miffin Harcourt Publishing Company, New York; (2015), 55

TAKE THE FIRST STEP

The story of Billy Mills' accomplishments is a story of using imagination that focuses on visualization. But to imagine is also to form an
image of something new that uses a step-by-step process, taking the first
step, then moving forward incrementally. To imagine this way creates
a new reality, one that doesn't depend on what is obvious now or what
others think. Mills knew what he wanted and did not limit himself by
what others defined as reasonable or possible: "If you limit your choice
only to what seems possible or reasonable, you disconnect yourself from
what you truly want, and all that is left is a compromise."[14]

· · ·

Over six years ago, I took a first step toward creating a new reality. I
had just completed a two-year physical therapist assistant program.
But my real desire was to be in a professional Feldenkrais training
program. I had just changed careers and had spent the money in my
retirement account to go to school. I needed to get to work. The
commitment to study the Feldenkrais Method required a four-year
time period, several thousand dollars in tuition each year, time off
from work three times a year amounting to seven weeks per year,
housing while out of town, travel from home for each segment, and
the purchase of equipment and books to use in my practice. Beside
all this, there was no training offered in Wyoming, the state I was
living in at the time, or in nearby Colorado, Utah, or anywhere else
that was feasible to attend. I felt that achieving this goal might not
be possible. It might just be beyond me. I felt I had to be practical
and responsible with our finances and the work that I chose.

14 Fritz, Robert; *The Path of Least Resistance: Learning to Become the Creative Force in Your Own Life;* Random House Publishing, New York, New York (1984)

But one day as I was doing a long run, I ran by the laundromat where I knew my wife was doing the week's laundry. I stopped in to say hi to her. She pulled out one of the local ad papers and showed me that a new training was starting in our area, in Boulder, Colorado. She said, "You have to do this." Now I had a decision to make. With Lee Ann's support, I decided to start the program.

Throughout the four years, she never wavered in her support. I not only started the program, but when it came time to pay for each of the twelve training segments, somehow, someway, we found the resources to pay for them so I could continue. As each segment passed, it became easier and easier to imagine completing the program. Looking back, finishing the program is still one of the most amazing things I have done. Many times, we looked at each other and wondered how it was possible we were making it on so little income, yet whenever more was needed, it appeared. We started with something that did not seem possible, but when it was achieved, it created a new idea of what could be. How fortunate that I had support and we believed in the impossible until it became possible.

What are your dreams?

• • •

Dreams

At night in the dark
Where freedom lies,
In dreams
In times of new creation
You wave the magic wand of gifts.
You are your deepest self.
You wander in all the realm and explore
Your power unlimited,
Your joy unfolding,

No artificial limits encumbering.
You walk your path searching for answers that will appear
Before morning comes.
You walk with lightness, even fly
Or sometimes labor to bring forth a new thing,
A new life.
But all the time there is a power, a fun
A knowing of awesomeness and security
Somewhere upholding.
Oh, what is sweeter than a dream?
You awake and find
That faith has grasped what is not seen.
Oh, what you dreamed does not yet appear,
It is not seen or felt or heard,
Logic does not make it appear.
It is only known, and with the eyes of knowing does now appear.
But what is this appearing and how does it show in doing,
But not in doing alone.
For doing is only a shadow I'm told of the dream,
Of the gift, of our personal goal,
And training is only a tool.
An artist cares only for the expression of art
Not so the factory.
For a dream is amorphous till we give it shape,
Yet a shape alone is boring.
Only some shapes are alluring, sensual, and preeminent
And true to the true form, the true form,
That is us in our dreams.
So, what is our doing and how do we do.
For quality and learning are the tools of true you.

. . .

Oh, what is sweeter than a dream realized!
Victory, arms raised in triumph, tears of joy.
For you have done it, you have waved that wand of gift
You stood true to your calling.
And now you have
A story of greatness to tell to all.
You have stayed the course, you have fought a good fight,
And no one can take that away from you.
You are you and more
For you are now more of you.

• • •

Oh, what is sweeter than a dream realized!
You dream and you dream
And back you go to a land that is even greater than then
And now it opens up oh so much more.
There is more here than I had seen before.
For greater power and ease and greater horizons appear.
For now, I know nothing,
Even less than before.
Now I am only beginning,
For I have just opened the door.
For now, I am pregnant once more,
And now I labor mightily again.
The joy, the expectation, the struggle, I have known before.
But the newness, the newness is greater still.
The wonder of dreams
Oh, what is sweeter than a new dream!

• • •

Think of at least one dream, one thing you want in life. Write it down if you wish. Write something specific and concrete. Set aside a few minutes to visualize this thing, this embodiment of your dreams. Then throughout each day, see the world through the eyes of the person you are, the one who is capable of living his or her dreams. When you write down specific things, you can employ the same process Billy Mills used to win an Olympic gold medal.

Our imaginations—which are a form of abstract thinking—set us apart from other animals. They define us as human. Our imaginations are the shapers of our intentions. Our imaginations become the starting point for this reshaping, this use of directed mental force. Our imagination is the most powerful, most basic, gentle, creative, and universal entry point into the process of true fitness.

Every human movement, even ones we cannot yet fully do, can be started, shaped, and nurtured using our imagination. Imagination is the key to developing true fitness. And fitness is the adapting of ourselves to our environments. The imagination provides a beginning point to improve movement, engage with the environment, experience fitness, or learn something new even at an old age. In the previous chapter, I talked about the idea of human abstract thinking, but no matter how clever humans are, they are nothing without a concomitant will to act. Our dreams are shaped in our imagination. Turning dreams into reality happens through the coupling of action with imagination and belief.

CHAPTER 3 LESSON:

IMAGINATION AND MOTION FOR IMPROVED MOVEMENT AND SELF-IMAGE

The use of the imagination is essential for self-improvement. In this case, organizing the back more powerfully and efficiently is an example of what imagination is capable of. You can use this lesson as an introduction to the power of imagination for improving both movement and the way you perceive yourself. If you cannot fully do a movement, you can imagine it. You will be surprised at how transformative the use of imagination is and how much change you will feel in yourself and the power and coordination of your back. There are many parts of ourselves that we're clearly aware of, such as our hands, fingertips, and lips. But most of us are not aware of all the parts of our backs. If you don't know where to begin something, start with your imagination. The objective is to use your imagination to engage with the lesson, not to do anything perfectly.

• • •

Take your time: Allow 30–40 minutes to complete this lesson the first time. Work through the lesson one part at a time. Try to complete the lesson in one session.

Part 1: Roll the Ball on the Back of Your Right Leg

1. Walk around slowly and sense the smoothness of your walking. Notice what you can about how your back contributes to your walking.

2. Lie on your stomach. Place one hand on top of the other, and rest your forehead on your hands. Begin by imagining a finger tracing a path along the back of your right calf from your heel to your knee. The pressure must be enough to allow you to feel your bones. Imagine the finger tracing the path from your right heel to your right knee many times until the path along the bones is very clear.

3. Now imagine an iron ball following the path traced by the finger. The ball rolls from the heel to the back of your right knee and back to your heel. Try to find all the points the ball would roll across to follow the path traced by the finger. To imagine this does not require movement.

4. Imagine the path of the ball continuing to roll from your right heel to your right knee and along your thigh until it comes to your buttocks. How the ball will roll across your buttocks is not clear. Try to imagine the spot the ball would roll to if your right leg was raised. Keep rolling the imaginary ball back and forth between your right heel and your buttocks until all the points along the path become clear.

· · ·

Part 2: Roll the Ball from Your Left Hand to Left Shoulder to Right Heel

1. Stretch out your left hand, leaving your forehead resting on the back of your right hand. Place the imaginary iron ball on the back of your left hand. Now imagine the path of the ball from the back of your left hand to your elbow and back. Trace this

path with the same imaginary finger you used in Part 1. Make sure this path is very clear. Continue to roll the ball all the way from your left hand to your elbow to your left shoulder blade. Note that at this point of transition, as the ball crosses your shoulder, the path of the ball is not clear.

2. Take your time. Thoroughly imagine the ball rolling from your left hand to your left shoulder.

3. Using your imagination, return the ball to your right heel. Stretch out your right foot and toes while leaving your heel pointing upwards. Raise your right heel slightly to roll the ball from your heel to your knee to your buttocks. Again, you are at a transition point, and the path of the ball is not yet clear. You will make the path of the ball clearer by finding the exact spot where the ball crosses the pelvis and then the spine on its way to your left shoulder. Roll the ball back on its course from your waist across your pelvis, buttocks, and knee to the heel. Continue rolling along this path until all the spots along the path are clear. Note the muscular activation in your left shoulder as you roll the ball up and across your buttocks.

4. In your imagination, return the ball to the back of your left hand. Lift your hand slightly, enough to cause the ball to roll from your hand to the elbow. Lift your elbow slightly to cause the ball to roll toward your left shoulder blade. Find the path the ball must take to cross your shoulder blade on its way to your spine. Roll the ball back to your elbow, up to your shoulder and onto your spine. Now roll the ball back down your spine, across your pelvis and buttocks, and back to your right heel.

5. Continue rolling the ball back and forth between your left hand and your right heel. To do this you must make sure that each point the ball travels to is lower than the point at which it currently sits. You must shape each part of your body to give the ball a smooth path. Make sure that you are aware of the exact location of the ball at all times. You may wonder if you are doing this "right." There is no right. The object is to pay attention to imagining the movement of the ball as exactly as you can at this moment and to notice the changes your attention produces.

6. Place the ball on your right heel. Lift your right leg slightly in order to start the ball rolling up your leg toward and across your buttocks. Roll the ball along your spine, and find the exact spot where the ball crosses your shoulder blade on the way toward your left arm. Go back and forth rolling the ball from your left hand to right heel by lifting first your left hand to start the ball rolling toward the shoulder on its path toward your right heel and then lifting your right leg to roll the ball back on its path toward your left hand.

7. Face your left ear on the floor, and straighten your left arm slightly. Raise your body in a way that allows the ball to travel in an imaginary groove from hand to heel and back again. Pay attention to the path of the ball.

8. Lift your left arm and right heel, then balance your body in a slightly arched position. Lift your arm and leg with light movements. Increase the amplitude of the movement until the ball rolls from hand to heel in one movement.

Take your time and explore thoroughly.

9. Come slowly to a standing position. Walk around and notice the difference between your left arm and right leg and the other pair (your right arm and left leg).

10. Lie down again on your stomach, and repeat Part 1 and Part 2, this time explore rolling the ball between your right hand and left leg.

. . .

Part 3: Roll the Ball on Your Centerline

1. Return to the floor and lie on your stomach. With your hands raised above your head and chin on the floor, roll the imaginary ball from your neck to your pelvis in the groove of your spine. To do this, raise your head and chest to start the ball rolling from your head down, then with your knees still on the floor, raise your pelvis to roll the ball back along its path toward the head. Do the rolling movements more slowly each time, taking time so you can notice the exact position of the ball at all times.

2. Spread your legs slightly and lift them just a little above the floor. Roll the ball from neck to pelvis with your legs lifted.

3. Now lower your legs and continue to roll the ball from neck to pelvis. Feel the difference between these two movements.

4. Raise your right arm and left leg, and roll the ball from your right hand to your left heel and back several times. Use light movement to roll it. Increase the amplitude of the movement each time until each movement ends with a bold swing.

5. Now raise your left arm and right leg, and roll the ball from your left hand to your right heel and back several times. Use light movement to roll it. Increase the amplitude of the movement each time until each movement ends with a bold swing.

6. Slowly come to a standing position.

7. Walk around. Does your back seem more organized now? Is your awareness of your back clearer?

. . .

In this lesson, you have filled in the parts of your back that were unclear to you by using your imagination. You have used movement to strengthen your imagination and used your imagination to unify movement. You have integrated movement and imagination and can use this tool powerfully in other lessons and in life. On a smaller scale, you used imagination and movement the way Billy Mills did. You've established a clearer self-image and better self-organization through the use of the imagination. How do you get from a known starting point (Point A) to a known ending point (Point B) when you don't know the territory in between? You do it through a combination of imagination and experiences. Can you feel that by using this kind of physical imagination you improved the strength, coordination, and use of your back and how you improved your acting in the world?

CHAPTER 4

Human Learning: Necessary Conditions for the Learning Process

Progress toward prosperity happens in times when I am quiet, when shelter is secure, when I observe the lion only from a distance. Here I can turn my attention to myself, and my skill of learning can flourish. Here I see what is needed and make new tools. I learn to use them with skill. A special combination of necessity, safety, quietness, curiosity, time, and desire drives me. I must have the right environment in which to learn, a quiet place with no distractions. Our cave home is that entry point, the essence of being human. Creativity grows here. The cave is part of my inner world, a place of comfort, the place where I create my inner and outer reality. In the cave I learn. I master. I solve. I move and act more effectively. I live more fully and powerfully in the world.

◄————————►

We must establish the right conditions if we are to progress. A quiet environment in which to learn is one of them. If the lion represents our fears (which are really self-limiting beliefs), then the cave represents a place where we are secure. It is a place where we revel in the joy of our potential, lay aside the need to achieve immediately, reduce the pressure of expectations, let go of the need to act by habit, reduce the physical effort expended, become more sensitive, unleash intuition, and are able to make the fine distinctions that make all the difference between almost there and Eureka, I've got it. It is always a joyful discovery to find that our new actions prove themselves in the environment. Such is the process of learning. It is a believing in oneself and in humanity and revealing what we are capable of. The cave is a place where believing in and acting on the process of being human are nurtured.

• • •

THE LEARNING PROCESS AS EXPLORATION

Learning is the key to human survival. Animals learn and humans learn. All animals including humans learn by the same process, the process of exploration. Animals explore their environment. They know where the watering holes are and where food is located. They can find shelter. They can navigate and find their way over the same terrain year after year. They know and remember dangers and avoid them. They even pass on some of what they have learned to their offspring, the next generation. In the same way, humans have a need to explore by moving into and learning about new territory. But there is one important difference: Humans are good at abstract thinking. Humans are capable of systematic explorations of new inward territory.

• • •

In his book *Arctic Dreams*, Barry Lopez says, "Human beings set out from places where they feel a sense of attachment, of shelter, and comprehension, and journey into amorphous spaces, characterized by a feeling of freedom or adventure, and the unknown. 'In open space,' writes Tuan, one can become intensely aware 'of (a remembered) place; and in the solitude of a sheltered place, the vastness of space acquires a haunting presence.' We must turn these exhilarating and sometimes terrifying new places into geography by extending the boundaries of our old places in an effort to include them. We pursue a desire for equilibrium and harmony between our familiar places and unknown spaces. We do this to make the foreign comprehensible or simply more acceptable.[15]"

But how do we explore? The process of exploration is one of sensing, feeling, noting, correlating, interrogating, connecting intimately with the environment around and within us. Lopez goes on to tell us that Eskimos are known to be able to navigate in polar darkness and whiteouts on barren featureless terrain by using the cues they have. They use the sounds of seabirds, the shape of the cracks in the ice, and the angle of the wind. The need to pay attention to the smallest cues is essential.[15]

In reality and metaphorically speaking, the need to explore new territory and develop our sensory awareness through exploration is apparent. Much of life is about gaining knowledge and practical experience and expanding our personal boundaries.

• • •

15 Lopez, Barry, *Arctic Dreams: Imagination and desire in a Northern Landscape*, Vintage Books, New York, (1986), 278

REFLECTION AND THE LEARNING PROCESS

What is it that you want? What is stopping you right now? In *A Life in Movement*, Moshe Feldenkrais summarizes the process of exploration, a process that starts with quieting the mind and proceeds toward focusing unhindered on the task at hand: "Self-examination and experimentation will reveal that everyone is naturally capable of being still, open, so attuned to a task that it can teach us and transform us into the way we need to be to find the optimal solution."[16]

Learning new mental skills follows the same process as learning physical skills. You learn to move objects and reorganize them in new ways. With time and experience, your ability to create and re-create increases.

I once worked with a young woman who didn't think she had the ability to take tests. She was particularly distressed because she didn't think she could pass the driver's license test. But when she laid aside the assumption that she could not pass a test and began to experiment by asking *what if* questions, she found a new capacity to learn. In order to find the answer to what lane she needed to be in to make a turn from a one-way street onto a two-way street, she looked at the diagram and began experimenting with what would happen if she turned into various lanes. Soon, she not only knew the answer to that question but discovered that her assumptions about herself were not correct. She'd combined the two qualities necessary for learning. She created the right environment by laying aside false assumptions and then she entered into the process of exploration, investigating all the possibilities.

---

16 *Moshe Feldenkrais: A Life in Movement*; Reese, Mark; Reese Kress Somatic Press, San Rafael, CA; copyright 2015.

You can be sure that your creativity, commitment, and connection to others will allow you to do what you want if you get false assumptions about your ability out of the way and follow the process of learning and exploring. If you become open to using what you have, you will find that you have at your disposal much more than you thought. If you get familiar with the learning process itself, you can learn anything.

They say that knowledge is power. But it is not knowledge alone that is powerful. Learning *how* to obtain real-world knowledge is what is powerful. We have access to knowledge about more than just things that are known. We can develop our ability to see underlying patterns and their benefits, which is the great human power. And the use of this power results in the true reward: learning how to learn.

CHAPTER 4 LESSON:
FIND YOUR LEARNING ZONE

As illustrated in the example of the cave, learning something new requires us to consciously create a quiet, non-stressful (physically and mentally) space. It doesn't require more effort. Effort destroys the sensitivity needed to notice the little things.

. . .

Take your time: Read through the lesson once, then allow 15 minutes to complete it.

1. Sit and look forward. Now, turn your head just a bit to the left and then back to center. Note how turning your head felt. Now, turn your head and neck to the left as far as is comfortable for you. Note how far that was and turn back to face forward. However far you turned your head, turn it half as much, and use half the effort. Many people cannot do this; they find it hard to turn only half as much and with less effort. When they turn, they look like they are going as far as they did the first time. Can you do it? Rest briefly.

2. Turn to the left again going half as far and with even less effort. Now you are turning only one quarter as much as the first turn. Rest.

3. Again, turn your head to the left but only one eighth as much as the first time and with even less effort.

4. Turn only your eyes to the left and then back to center. Turn the eyes half as much and then one quarter as much and then one eighth as much to the left. Rest briefly.

5. Turn your head and neck slowly to the left as much as you did the first time. Is it easier this time?

• • •

If you were truly able to reduce the effort each time, then you probably noticed some improvement, especially regarding ease of motion. This is the learning environment that we want to create and use. We have more of ourselves, more of our innate abilities open to us in this state of reduced effort and relaxed focus.

Removing the stress of achieving, of turning far, allows you to learn to do the movement better, more efficiently. Reducing the effort by being in a place that supports focus without the distraction of the stress of assuming that moving and learning must be hard is where we learn best. This is *the zone of improvement*, our starting point. Failing to realize our potential is most often caused by limiting assumptions about our ability to overcome difficult tasks. Moving easily and removing the pressure to achieve quickly are a powerful first step in the learning process.

CHAPTER 5

Survival and Fitness: It Is Always about Movement

I am a human. I am weak compared to other animals, small compared to the largest predators, and very slow moving. I climb hills slowly and have poor traction on slick surfaces and no tough pads on my feet. My high center of gravity makes it easy to knock me off my feet. My sense of smell and hearing are not equal to many other mammals. I have no natural weapons: no large teeth, no claws, no fur to protect me. Worse, I carry my vulnerable belly and throat in plain sight in front of me, completely exposed when I stand upright. I wonder if I will survive. Despite my failings, despite my weaknesses, despite my poor odds of surviving, I do have a few characteristics that are helpful.

And tomorrow we must have meat. I am an equatorial animal. I have learned to cover myself in animal skins when it is cold. I am a puny hunter, but I have a few advantages. My upright stance frees my hands for action. My heel cord is a huge elastic band that stores energy when I run. I have large, round muscles that connect the backside of my legs to my bony midsection. I feel these muscles stabilizing and propelling me when I run. I have noticed that apes do not have these muscles. They have a flat butt and are not able to walk upright.

I am the only predator on the plains that sweats profusely. When I sweat, I stay cooler on hot days. Because I don't have fur, I don't trap heat around myself. I can carry water with me. I am not fast, but I have great endurance. I have another unique feature. My upright stance and unique shoulder girdle give me the ability to rotate around a vertical axis, and my spine and hips allow me to throw objects accurately. No other animal can throw as many different kinds of objects as precisely and powerfully as I can.

I will hunt antelope. I have learned from knowledge passed on to me how to hunt in my own style. I hunt with others, and I communicate in more sophisticated ways than other animals. I sharpen sticks and make effective spears. I reflect on and continually improve my tools. I eat both plants and animals. I devise clever strategies.

The Sun is high in the sky; the temperature is rising. It is time to hunt. Antelope are much faster than I am, but their endurance is short on this hot day. I take five clan members, and we set out toward the watering hole where we know the antelope are. We head toward one and drive it from the herd. The entire herd runs. Our antelope outruns us and returns to the herd. But we know which one we are chasing. We jog toward it again. Again, it runs. Again, we chase.

Our antelope is finally separated from its herd. He runs far away and we track. He runs again and again. The antelope is overheating in the hot sun. I am getting exhausted. I am overheating. I come close to heat sickness. I am pushing the limits of endurance. I need to keep on. The antelope and I are locked in a struggle; we share a moment of life and death. Our spirits are joined. I lose the prey and find him again. I enter his mind and become one with his struggle. When I lose him, I stop and feel, feel the pursuit. I feel the direction I must flee, and when I enter the antelope's struggle, I feel what he feels. I see the terrain as he sees it and sense his strength and feel his decisions. I know the way, and I follow again. I do this for hours. I drink from the water my companions are carrying. I am the appointed one today. I am the best runner. I will finish tracking our prey. The antelope clings to life and flees.

I use my mind to be the antelope; I become the prey. I am in his mind, and I sense where he is hiding. I find him again. He flees, yet I see him failing in strength. I must persist or all has been for naught. Both of us are caught in this struggle.

Finally, the antelope falls. He has resisted to the end, but now he is on the verge of death. I see the look in his eyes as he surrenders his spirit, and I am sad. I come near and drive my spear into him. I lay my head on my dead prey's neck and give thanks. I praise the animal's character and courage. My friends have caught up with me. Our stone knives go to work. We rejoice and give thanks for the gift the antelope has given us. On the plains, I am the ultimate endurance athlete. We will eat today, and we will live. We eat as other predators do; we are like all the other animals.

On the one hand, humans are inherently frail. On the other hand, a three thousand-year-old pictograph in Matobo National Park, Zimbabwe shows images of runners in full stride, which highlights one of humanity's greatest potential strengths, the gift of persistence. Designated runners in many Native-American cultures would run down deer, antelope, and moose. Endurance walking and running have played a large part in the human story. Before horses the only way to get around was on two feet. And migration and transportation are essential.

As late as the 1950s, Navajo runners were still running deer to exhaustion.[17] And during the height of the Inca empire, Inca messengers could cover 150 miles per day in a relay system.[18] The Apache were known to be able to cover 50–75 miles per day and run for several days at a time.[19]

Researcher Daniel Lieberman has theorized that the need for humans to run long distances was a key factor in human evolution.[20] His theories are difficult to prove. Whether Lieberman's theories are correct, it is clear that movement shaped the evolutionary develop-ment of man.

Many attempts have been made to duplicate primitive man's ability to run prey to death. Scott Carrier, who wrote the memoir *Running After Antelope*, describes his attempts to run down antelope on the plains of Wyoming. Carrier attempted many times to run antelope to exhaustion. He was never able to accomplish the task. Why not?

As it turns out, running ability is not the only requirement. Carrier describes how the antelope would return to the herd, making it difficult for the runner to locate the one he'd been chasing because the antelope all looked the same to human eyes. When runners did keep an antelope from returning to the herd, the antelope would use the terrain to its advantage to lose its pursuers.[21]

17 Heinrich, Bernd; *Racing the Antelope: What Animals Can Teach Us About Running and Life;* Harper Collins; New York, New York (2001)

18 History.com staff, "Inca," History.com, A+E Networks (2015), http://www.history.com/topics/inca

19 Milroy, Andy; *North American Ultrarunning A History;* JMD Media (2012)

20 Lieberman, Daniel E. and Dennis M. Bramble, "The Evolution of Marathon Running: Capabilities in Humans" Sports Medicine (2007) 37(4-5): 288- 290.

21 Carrier, Scott; *Running After Antelope;* Counterpoint, Washington DC; (2001)

Being able to run a long distance on a hot day was not enough to run down an antelope. Running down an antelope on a hot day is so difficult that the theory of persistence hunting being a factor in human evolution was not accepted at first. This is because it is difficult to find people who use this method of hunting. But Louis Liebenberg, author of *The Art of Tracking*, spent time living among the Kalahari tribe of central Africa, who are still skilled in this technique, and witnessed a persistence hunt firsthand. And, David Attenborough's documentary *The Life of Mammals* shows Kalahari bushmen running down a kudu.[22]

Liebenberg examines the principles of tracking used by the Kalahari. He explains three very different kinds of tracking skills. The first skill is recognizing the tracks of different animals. The second skill involves more than distinguishing between the tracks of various insects and animals. It integrates knowledge of the animals' habits. The ability to fill in the gaps when signs are not continuously present is necessary to track prey.

The ability to enter an animal's experience, to join with the animal's mind to form a hypothesis, is the third type of tracking called speculative tracking. This skill requires great intellectual capability in order to form a hypothesis and test it. It requires a good deal of creative ability and even the ability to be intuitive or empathic. Liebenberg suggests that this kind of abstract creative thought is the foundation of science and is not a different process than that used by modern theoretical physicists.[23]

---

22 Attenborough, David; "The Life of Mammals: Food for Thought", BBC (August 2017) Volume 10, http://www.bbc.co.uk/programmes/b007c1vc

23 Liebenberg, Louis; *The Art of Tracking: The Origin of Science*; David Phillip Publishers, South Africa; (1990)

Now we have examples of movement: the movement of running and the movement of the mind in tracking. What we think of as mental activity and what we tend to think of as physical activity are actually the same thing. Both are types of movement. One moves the body through space while the other senses, feels, and connects with the environment and moves ideas and concepts around. Man's ability to survive is based on these two types of movement.

Persistence hunting is a whole-person, mind-body activity. Already we have fundamental concepts and understandings of fitness that we can summarize.

Now we know about and feel the special gift we have for movement, the gift for persistence. We can outrun a swift animal over time, but it is the second type of movement—mental movement—that empowers the first and makes persistence hunting possible. It projects a unified mind and body that feeds our bellies and makes us truly human.

The antelope was run to its death on a hot day but was not killed by strength or speed. Humans used the animal's strengths and weaknesses against itself. They observed and understood their prey and knew the prey's abilities. They hunted by working together as a clan.

Fitness is a practical mind-body experience in which persistence plays a part and sensory awareness is in high demand. Fitness is inherently practical. Mindless chasing does not produce a meal.

CHAPTER 5 LESSON:
THE DIFFERENCE BETWEEN WALKING AND RUNNING

Fitness is always about movement, not mindless movement but movement improved through awareness.

Many people shuffle when they run. They swing their leg forward but do not pick it up in front. Picking the knee up with the psoas muscle is part of getting both feet off the ground at once. As your back foot and leg come into a position of hip extension and then leave the ground, your front foot is also raised above the ground in a kind of marching movement, and you are propelled forward briefly with both feet off the ground. How much you lift depends on how fast you are running, what kind of terrain you are on, and what you are doing with the rest of your body.

Many people think that running is just another form of walking. Some people's running looks like a form of walking. But running and walking are different movements. This lesson will help you experience the difference between the two. It will also help you coordinate lifting your foot with the actions of your knees with the turning of your pelvis and spine.

When we walk, we often move our foot a bit in front of our knee and follow through from heel to toe. Your walking may be more or less this way. But when walking, we always have at least one foot on the ground. The rear foot guides the movement before being lifted from the ground and brought forward. The front foot makes contact with the ground and then begins to move backward. There is no float phase in walking where both feet are off the ground. Walking does not require you to organize yourself to "land under your hips." Walking and running both use the skeleton well, but they use the muscles differently. In this lesson, you'll feel this different use of the muscles and joints as you alternate between walking and marching.

· · ·

Take your time: Allow 30–45 minutes to complete this lesson.

1. Take off your shoes, and walk around using your normal walking pattern. How does your walking feel? Are you walking heel first and then bringing your toe down (heel-toe-heel-toe), or are you doing something else? What are you doing with your pelvis? Is it moving? There are many ways to walk. If you were walking on a very rough or gravelly surface, would you walk heel to toe?

2. Switch from walking to lifting your leg with a bent knee in a marching pattern. Go back and forth between walking and marching. Switch back and forth many times, but make the transition between walking and marching slower each time. Feel the differences in each pattern. As you move more slowly, see if you can feel the areas in which your muscles are working. Can you do the walking and marching movements with minimal effort?

3. Alternate between the two movements at different speeds. Go very slowly and then a little faster. Pay attention to the differences. Experiment with different heights as you raise your bent knee. Raise your knee until your foot is only inches off the floor and then try raising it to different heights but not higher than having your thigh parallel to the floor.

Notice that in the marching motion, your quads can be relatively inactive. They are resting as you lift your knee. When you're walking, the quads can be activated to straighten the leg to a greater or lesser degree when swinging it forward. Many muscles work together in the walking motion. The action of lifting the knee involves the hip flexor muscles in a special way and de-emphasizes the action of the leg muscles in a special way.

In fact, the action of lifting your bent knee is accomplished not by the muscles you might usually think of as leg muscles but by your strongest hip flexor: the iliopsoas musculature. This is a muscle whose tendon inserts very high and on the inside of the femur, or thigh bone, just below the hip joint. The psoas complex originates on the inside of the pelvis and the vertebrae of the lumbar and thoracic spine L5 at the junction of the spine to the pelvis and to T12 at the lower end of the ribcage. This is the strongest hip flexor in the body and one of the strongest muscles in the body. Unlike many other skeletal muscles, this muscle cannot be seen because it is covered by the muscles of the belly wall.

The psoas muscle is engaged when walking but is very important in marching. Become aware of the action of this powerful hip flexor and where it takes place by feeling its action as you lift a bent knee.

4. Return to marching. Do it more slowly. Slow down even more. Hold your lifted knee in the air for a second or two. Can you feel something happening deep in your belly high above your hips?

Outdoor Option

1. Warm up and then gently begin to run in place. Run lightly as if marching in place. Lift one bent knee, and let it gently come back to the ground. Lift the other knee, and let it gently come

down. Alternate left/right, left/right. Go slowly at first and then let the movement of lifting be smaller, lighter, and quicker while marching in place.

2. Rest in a standing position.

3. March in place again. As you do, let the movement of lifting your knees get smaller and smaller until you come to a stop.

4. Once again, march/run in place. Lean your whole postural column forward and begin to slowly run.

5. Pick up speed and run normally.

Do you have a new normal after doing this lesson? See if this lesson has any effect on your running. The running movement occurs mainly in the core musculature: the glutes, hamstrings, psoas, and the coordinated action of the muscles in your body's trunk that act on the pelvis. Can you make this an easy, whole-body movement pattern? Can you integrate this new idea of lifting so that it does not dominate but harmonizes with the rest of the action of your core muscles? The idea is not to lift high but to clearly and softly distinguish between shuffling by pushing the feet forward and running: This involves lightly lifting the feet. You can practice this lesson anytime to sharpen your awareness of the difference between walking and running.

CHAPTER 6

Fitness as Self-Fulfillment: Beyond Survival

I am now a human living on the great open grasslands. I have little size and strength compared with other predators. I respect the lion. The lion shows courage when he attacks the bison with its deadly horns. The lion shows wisdom when he sizes up the fight. I admire the lion, yet he strikes terror in our hearts.

In my life I have seen a man, my friend, in the jaws of a lion. My friend screamed as he was bitten over and over. It was a terrifying shriek, agonizing, one that you cannot know unless you have heard. Not a quick cry but a lingering scream, the agony of death itself, food for my worst nightmares.

And now the lion challenges us again. A lion came into our camp last night and silently stole one of our children. We know this lion; it threatened us before and took some of our cattle. Now I have lost a little one, a son, and I grieve. My heart aches, and anger fills me. We mourn, but we also reflect. I am an animal, the same as all others, but I am also a man, a human. We have no choice but to accept the challenge.

We adapt. We make tools to augment our strength and hunt the mighty lion, but that is not enough. We also cultivate courage; we must find it within ourselves to face the lion. We plan what we must do tomor-

row. Tomorrow we will hunt the lions. We will kill the lion that killed our child. We will hunt together as a group, as one and many. In the early dawn we gather. We form a line, holding our spears, jumping high in the air, and chanting in unison. We focus our eyes straight ahead; our hearts race faster. Our voices become louder as we focus our emotions. We forget our fears and control our thoughts: the lion, the lion, the lion.

We track the lion by watching overhead for vultures that will alert us of fresh lion kill. I spot the lion in the open plain feasting on fresh meat. Our group is a fearsome sight as we jog elegantly straight for the lion who is not used to being driven from his kill. The lion eyes us and reluctantly walks away. He is alone on the open plain.

We run after him. I am the first to throw a spear. My spear lodges deep in the lion's side, and we close on him. The wounded lion slows in the heat. I have another spear. I thrust it into the lion, pushing it into him with controlled passion, with intent to kill and compassion all at once. The lion is down. We all come near and finish him with many thrusts of our spears. I respect the lion, but now I have seen terror in the eyes of the mighty. The predator turned prey. We will eat well, for our children and even our livestock are protected now. We have avenged our child.

Tonight, we will dance, sing, and celebrate into the night. Our voices will be heard high above the flames of the campfire. Our hearts are set free. Our spirits are renewed. Our children are safe.

By adapting, we prey on the predator, we begin to rule our environment. Fitness is, in essence and by definition, the ability to adapt. Fitness is about staying alive and much more; it is the joy of living by overcoming obstacles. Learning is the key to thriving, and to thrive is to celebrate.

So, it is that at all times and in all cultures, true fitness changes our self-image and defines our place in the environment. Celebrating life is an expression of fitness. Barry Lopez in *Arctic Dreams* makes the same observation of the Eskimo people: They have a quality of *nuannaarpoq*; they take extravagant pleasure in being alive, and they delight in finding it in others.[24]

A more modern example of life-affirming fitness is from clinical rotations when I was in physical therapist assistant training. In the middle of one of my last clinical experiences, things were not going well. I was in a new environment and having trouble adapting. The setting was busy and chaotic. I needed to do well, and the feedback I was getting made me question whether I could succeed. After a full week, the weather turned rainy, and I had scheduled an interval workout for that Friday.

I showed up to the track in pouring rain, warmed up, and completed the workout. The rain came down hard enough that it was difficult to see. When I was done, I had accomplished something so physical and pure that my spirit was renewed, my belief in myself had been strengthened. I celebrated a good moment in life and went on to pass my clinical. The effort produced a reward. Haven't we all experienced moments like this? This kind of fitness, this adaptation, is a gateway to life, not a drudgery to be born. I call it biological fitness as opposed to the narrow realm of physical fitness. Biological fitness is organic fitness. Organic fitness means that what is inherent within the individual has been expressed: the individual proclivities, interests, personality, and expression of spirit. Biological fitness is life affirming.

24 Lopez, Barry; *Arctic Dreams: Imagination and Desire in a Northern Landscape*; Vintage Books, New York (1986), 202

CHAPTER 6 LESSON:

THE UNIVERSAL HUMAN POSITION OF TRIUMPH AND CELEBRATION

Sometimes someone will tell me that they cannot do a movement lesson because they have pain or other limitations. When that is the case, it is perfectly fine to visualize an entire lesson or part of a lesson rather than to do the physical movements. In this lesson, I suggest doing minute movements or to simply imagine—visualize—doing a movement. Don't be confused by this; you may do either.

Please work through this lesson one part at a time doing each part slowly. The purpose of this lesson is to understand that self-fulfillment is expressed in movement.

· · ·

Take your time: Allow 30–40 minutes to complete this lesson.

Part 1: Hip and Shoulder Circles

1. Lie on your left side with both knees and hips bent at 90-degree angles, as if you were sitting in a chair. Stack your knees. Place your left hand in any position that is comfortable. Like you did with your knees, stack your top foot on top of your bottom foot.

2. Perform a miniscule movement by taking your top knee just in front of your bottom knee in a direction that takes the knee farther in front of yourself. Keep your top foot stacked on top of your bottom foot. Can you feel which vertebrae move to bring

your top knee forward a small amount? Do this movement in a very easy manner until it becomes clear and easy to do.

3. Now move your top knee backward a tiny amount. This is a different movement. Can you feel how your back moves now? Can you feel how and where the movement originated? Do this movement a number of times.

4. Rest on your back.

5. Come back to a position on your side with knees bent and stacked. Stack your feet. Maintain this position, and move your top hip slightly closer to your top shoulder and then move your top hip a little farther from your top shoulder. Do this several times.

6. Make tiny circles with your top hip. The circles will be in a plane that is parallel to the floor. Feel how the muscles of your back, sides, and the front of your torso work together to make these circles. Move only slightly or simply visualize doing the movements. Do the circles in the other direction. See how circular they can become.

7. Rest on your back.

8. Return to the position on your side. Bend your top arm at a 90-degree angle. Ball up your hand into a loose fist. Begin to make tiny, gentle circles with your top shoulder or visualize the movement.

9. Now add hip circles. Do both circles together a number of times and then change the direction of one of the circles.

10. Rest and then lie on your other side with your knees and hips bent at 90-degree angles like you did before. Repeat the hip and shoulder circles.

11. Stand and bend both arms at 90-degrees angles. Ball your hands into loose fists. Imagine that there is something circular about the hips and shoulders as you lightly swing your arms and walk. Don't force anything. Don't try to make circles. Allow the idea of circular hips to be in the back of your mind. Walk around the room and sense how your walking is.

Part 2: Arms above Your Head

In this next set of movements, you do not need to have your hands or arms on the floor. Just make sure you are comfortable. You can bend your wrist backward letting only the fingertips touch the floor, or you can stack pillows under your arms if need be.

1. Return to the floor and lie on your back. Raise both arms above your head. You may or may not be able to rest your arms on the floor above your head. Work within your comfort zone.

2. Bend both knees and place the soles of both feet flat on the floor with your lower legs more or less vertical. Press your feet into the floor, lift your hips, and feel whether your hands travel farther along the floor over your head and away from your feet. Now, imagine the twelve vertebrae in your thoracic (chest) area and five vertebrae in your low back area.

3. Being very careful to stay in your comfort zone and resting whenever necessary, begin to lower yourself to the floor one vertebra at a time. Go slowly enough to take a breath as you lower each vertebra. Notice how you have to shape yourself to lower each. Use your imagination to feel each vertebra. Can you feel your shoulder blades move over your ribs and how they change position each time you adjust yourself? Keep your arms

and shoulders supported, but notice if your arms have changed position in relation to your torso.

4. Bring everything down and rest. Rest with your legs straight and arms at your sides.

5. Repeat this process several times. Your goal is only to make the movement easier each time. Go very slowly, and rest on your back between each repetition.

Part 3: Arm Overhead with Knees Tilted

1. Bend your knees and let both knees tilt slightly to the right. Raise your left arm comfortably overhead and away from your feet. Support your arm as needed. Turn your head a little to the left.

2. Breathe. Sense the movement and expansion between your lowest pair of ribs. At the same time, sense the contact of the right side of your rib cage with the floor. Continue to breathe, and notice the expansion between each pair of ribs on your left side until you notice the expansion of the last ribs under your armpit and collarbone. Do each movement gently, pleasantly.

3. Rest.

4. Repeat on the other side. This time raise your right arm, and tilt your knees slightly to the left.

5. Rest again.

6. One more time, raise both arms overhead. Raise your pelvis until you feel weight on the C7 vertebra, the one at the base of your neck. Lower slowly noticing the contact of each vertebra.

7. Rest on your back a final time with your arms and legs stretched long.

Part 4: The Universal Expression of Victory

1. After completing Part 3, roll to one side, and come to a standing position. Walk around the room using the imaginary rolling of the hips and shoulders that you did in the first part of this lesson.

2. Walk around the room a couple of times while imagining that you are going somewhere. Then imagine that you just crossed a finish line, passed a critical test, threw a touchdown pass, or reached the summit of a mountain. What would be a universal movement that symbolizes triumph and the joy of accomplishment, a movement understood around the world and throughout time?

3. Raise your arms gently into the air overhead and celebrate with a gesture that requires no words.

• • •

I hope that Section 1 of this book and the accomplishments you've experienced as you've worked through the lessons have made you feel triumphant and set your expectation for the sections that follow.

Figure 6.1. The author on top of the Matterhorn, in the Alps of Oregon

SECTION 2

HOW SCIENCE HELPS US
UNDERSTAND HUMAN POTENTIAL

CHAPTER 7

In the Beginning There Was Belief

Section 1 began at the beginning, with a blank slate, with the words from Genesis One, "and the earth was without form and void." It describes the continual organization of life on Earth until it reached the human animal, the animal that developed a new kind of thinking ability. Section 1 defined human fitness in terms of our relationship to the physical environment.

In Section 2, let's begin again from an entirely different starting point, a conceptual viewpoint rather than an evolutionary one, and see how modern science helps us to understand human fitness.

What can we learn about human adaptation and improvement from a conceptual viewpoint? Look at the sentence from John 1:1, "In the beginning was the word": *logos*, from whence we get "logic," an organizing principle. This familiar quote implies that in the beginning, at the start of something, we might find a basic organizing principle. What might this be, and where is our starting point? In terms of human aspirations and human self-organization or self-reorganization, the beginning is faith—or confidence. Like Bruce Lee said, "The possession of anything begins in the mind."[25]

• • •

25 Lee, Bruce; Bruce *Lee Jeet Kune Do*, Tuttle Publishing, North Clarendon Vermont (1997), Section 6: Beyond System

CONFIDENCE

The words "believe" and "confidence" come from similar roots. To believe is to accept something as true, and confidence is to trust in someone or something.[26] Self-confidence then is trust in yourself. Self-confidence is not just a mental quality. It is something that inspires great action. How could primitive man have had the confidence—the extreme boldness—to use a spear to take down a lion or even a woolly mammoth, an animal that weighed 6 tons? When you stop to think about it, this kind of confidence is audacious. What can explain this kind of belief? The answer to this question is contained in something that is common across the animal kingdom. All animals are confident in the performance of their species-specific abilities.

To understand this, watch a video of a cheetah chasing or a lion stalking its prey. You will see that these animals are very comfortable as they exhibit their hunting abilities. A cheetah, the fastest land animal, has no trouble knowing and feeling that it can run fast. It is an innate ability, something inherent in its species. The mature eagle experiences no inner turmoil when hopping off a cliff and soaring in the wind. The eagle has the innate ability to fly. Humans also have innate abilities. We have the ability to sense and feel the power of our superior abstract thinking abilities and thus know that we can outsmart our prey. Our ability to think in highly abstract ways is the basis for human confidence.

There are two things involved here. First, and just as the eagle cannot fly immediately after hatching from the egg, we cannot use all our abilities immediately. Birds are born with the *potential* to fly, and humans have the innate ability to learn beyond that which any

---

26 Strong, James; *Strong's Exhaustive Concordance of the Bible*, Hendrickson Publishers (2007)

other animal can. Second, there is the aspect of mastery of what is innate through experience.

There is an aspect of beauty, comfort, and enjoyment in using innate abilities. That is, acknowledging and enjoying our potential before we begin to learn a new skill. This is the basic unblocked confidence of a child or of a champion. Then there is the increase in confidence that comes from acting on potential and progressing toward mastery of something.

But what does science say about human belief? You can believe in yourself, in your innate human abilities, and apply belief to the task at hand. I am not speaking just of positive thinking but a general mindset about what our abilities are and what we can accomplish. How do we know that belief is so critical to our success in life?

. . .

WE BECOME WHAT WE THINK

There has been much research conducted lately regarding the science of belief. The positive and healing effects of the placebo effect have been well documented, and recent research has shown that thinking something will happen has an effect on the body's chemistry, specifically on neuropeptides. *Neuro* because they usually exist in the brain and *peptide* because they are proteins. One neuropeptide most people have heard of is endorphin. Athletes are familiar with endorphins. The body's release of chemical endorphins results in what's known as a runner's or exercise high and helps to block pain. Neuropeptides are associated with a host of bodily functions. There are receptors all over the body. Emotions result in neuropeptide production, and neuropeptide production results in emotions and even in the improvement of thought. It is a two-way street. Every thought or emotion produces a result in the body, and every action in the body produces emotion.[27] It is also now known that the brain and immune system are intricately linked.[28] We become our thoughts; our thoughts influence our health. We now know that even genes require input to function. As James Allen says, "The aphorism, 'As a man thinketh in his heart so is he' not only embraces the whole of a man's being, but is so comprehensive as to reach out to every condition and circumstance of his life."[29]

. . .

BELIEF AFFECTS OUTCOMES

Belief is the framework on which hang all our thoughts, feelings, and actions. Belief not only shapes these things, it affects our outcomes in life. Carol Dweck, who has spent decades researching the value of mindsets, tells us in her book *Mindset: The New Psychology of Success* that two distinct mindsets exist, and they affect all areas of our lives.[30] There is the fixed mindset in which intelligence and ability do not change: We are stuck with what we have and are obligated to prove that we have enough of these qualities. In the second

---

27 Hamilton, David R., *It's the Thought That: Why Mind Over Matter Really Works,* Hay House Inc. Introduction and Chapters 1 and 2.

28 Louveau, Antonie and Igor Smirnov, et al: *Structural and Functional Features of Central Nervous System Lymphatic Vessels,* Nature: International Weekly Journal of Science (July 16, 2013) 523, 337-331. doi:10.1038/nature14432

29 Allen, James, written in contemporary language by Charles Conrad, *As a Man Thinketh, 21ˢᵗ Century Edition,* Best Success Books (2017)

30 Dweck, Carol S, PhD., Mindset: *The New Psychology of Success; Ballentine,* New York; (2016)

mindset—the growth mindset—we realize that life is a continual process of growth and nothing about us is static.

These two mindsets profoundly affect the outcomes of our lives. One leads to lifelong learning and expansion of abilities. The other avoids challenges and remains only interested in things that are already easy. Other studies have shown that mindset interventions aimed at changing the participant's outlook from the easy road to one more accepting of stress and challenge can be a catalyst and that even a one-hour intervention can continue to have an effect on a person for years.

In *The Upside of Stress*, researcher Kelly McGonigal shares a story of a 30-minute intervention for 120 freshmen who attended high school in a low-income area near the San Francisco Bay. The intervention focused on empowering the young people by highlighting their ability to change who they were over time. The impact was amazing. At the end of the year, 81 percent of the students passed ninth-grade algebra as compared to only 58 percent of the control group, and GPAs rose to 2.6 as opposed to only 1.6 in the control group. Clearly, science confirms that what we think and believe is a critical factor in how our life evolves.[31]

· · ·

BELIEF IS A CHOICE

Nothing in the arena of self-improvement or living our dreams happens without the belief that it can happen. Ultimately, belief is a

---

31 McGonigal, Kelly, PhD: *The Upside of Stress: Why Stress is Good for You and How to Get Good at It*; Penguin Random House, 375 Hudson Street, New York, New York 10014 (2015)

choice. Henry Ford is credited with saying, "If you believe you can do something or if you believe you can't, you are right."[32]

Belief is the choice that starts the learning process, a process of increased self-awareness. Awareness—the highest level of human functioning—is the key to learning how to be in touch with our innate abilities, our innate confidence. Which mindset will you choose? Will it be the mindset of a victim, always comparing yourself unfavorably to outside circumstances, or will it be the mindset of the predator, the one who is more than equal to the challenges of living?

The spear—and courage and skill it took to use it—made us more than equal to the lion. Innovation, emotional focus, practice, and patience all work together as a result of a growth mindset. The result is the integration of the whole person into the concept of fitness.

We cannot afford to think negatively about our abilities. While a positive mindset toward stress and challenge doesn't mean we will always get everything we want, it does mean that we can direct the progress of our growth and make the most of all life's opportunities. And don't forget another element that helped primitive man survive: the ability to persist, a belief that he was equipped to outlast the animal he was chasing or the situation he was challenged with. Persistence is the power to see things through because we have belief and hope. Belief with persistence creates the realities of your life. This becomes an extraordinary thing, a human thing. It is the ability to transcend. The challenge becomes a doorway to human elevation in the environment. This is fitness.

• • •

32 1947 September, The Reader's Digest, Volume 51, (Filler item), Quote Page 64, The Reader's Digest Association. (Verified on paper) https://quoteinvestigator.com/2015/02/03/you-can/#note-10545-1

BELIEF CAN BE PRACTICED

Learn to believe. Yes, we can think of belief or confidence as a skill we can learn and practice. A child does not yet know how not to be confident in his innate ability to learn. And a champion can practice confidence. But what is confidence, and how do we understand and practice security and trust? In Section 1, I presented an element of security, the cave home. We can also call it the *boma*, a word of Swahili origin. A boma is an enclosure made of thorn bushes. It protects livestock and small camps by creating a barrier between them and predators. It is a boundary that helps to control the environment.

Once we have established boundaries, we have a chance to flourish. Inside boundaries fright can be transformed into anxiety, anxiety can be transformed into challenge, and challenge can be motivating and exciting. Relative quietness can allow us to consider creative solutions to problems. So, personal security is a prerequisite for the growth of confidence and belief. But sometimes people stop at the idea of security. The idea of security on the savanna was to create an environment that would allow humanity to find solutions. This is a different idea than being perfectly safe. The skilled use of the spear made mankind equal to the lion, but spears were by no means perfectly safe to use.[33] To seek perfect safety is to stop the

---

33 Wilkins, Jayne and Benjamin J. Schoville, et al., *An Experimental Investigation of the Functional Hypothesis and Evolutionary Advantage of Stone-Tipped Spears,* PLoS One (August 27, 2014), doi: 10.1371/journal.pone.0104514 https:// www.ncbi.nlm.nih.gov/pmc/articles/PMC4146534/. Stone-tipped spears have been shown to increase the size of a wound cavity deep inside the animal, giving a greater likelihood of organ damage and a higher probability of lethality than untipped spears, decreasing the need to stay in close proximity to the animal and deliver multiple spear thrusts. This upgrade in primitive technology required great cognitive ability. Primitive spears were lethal, and they worked on a similar idea to modern expanding bullets.

growth process and settle for being a victim in an ever-changing world. Security and personal boundaries are a platform on which we can build more confidence.

Dr. Feldenkrais described his aim as helping people to "live their avowed and unavowed dreams."[34] To live an unavowed dream means to live something that has not been put into words, something that you are not consciously aware of but that exists deep within you. It is to be in harmony with yourself, to be secure within your own skin. The purpose of security is to produce harmony, not absolute safety. Obstacles reveal the nature of our insecurities.

How do we practice confidence and security to live our dreams? Sports psychologist Dr. Bob Rotella, in his book *How Champions Think*, states that he teaches his golfers to prepare for the competition before the tournament by focusing only on their performance once they begin play. He teaches them that the most crucial element of competition is focusing on mastering their inner game. He recommends that clients do two types of practice. First, he has them visualize success. He tells of making highlight "videos" that athletes can watch at the end of each day in which they see themselves succeeding at their sport or succeeding at improving a particular skill. This first type of practice develops the innate confidence in our human abilities and in our ability to express and develop them. Second, Dr. Rotella describes a practice of continuous work to develop the mental or motor skills necessary to do what the athlete wants to do. He describes instructing LeBron James to make 200, 3-point shots off a dribble and 200 catch-and-shoot 3-pointers every day. That is

---

34 Feldenkrais, Moshé, "Embodied Wisdom: The Collected Papers of Moshe Feldenkrais," Good Reads (2017) https://www.goodreads.com/work/quotes/16277244-embodied-wisdom-the-collected-papers-of-moshe-feldenkrais

a lot of practice. But LeBron stuck with it and increased his 3-point shooting accuracy by over 30 percent.[35] In both of these types of practice, confidence can be learned and improved. Belief is a decision about how we choose to see ourselves.

How can you improve your commitment to believing in yourself in the same way these athletes do?

35 Rotella, Bob, *How Champions Think,* Simon and Shuster, New York (2015) 8

CHAPTER 7 LESSON:
TWO KINDS OF CONFIDENCE

We become what we believe, so this lesson focuses on the mind-body connection. This lesson is a beginning, and when we begin something, it pays to ask questions. You may return to this lesson time and again as needed.

· · ·

Take your time: Allow 30–40 minutes to complete this lesson.

1. Lie down on the floor and ask yourself four questions:

    a. What do I like?

    b. What do I want?

    c. What am I interested in?

    d. How can the answer to the first three questions help me find satisfaction in life and be of service to others?

    Take as long as you would like to contemplate these questions. Don't try to figure out any answers; just listen quietly to how you feel about each of these questions. At the present time, you might feel that you know what you want, or you may find these questions hard to answer. To truly know what we want is difficult, and you will return to these questions many times in life. But after meditating on these four questions, you probably have at least a powerful inkling, the beginning of answers to each of the questions.

2. Get up and walk around for a few moments, then come back and lie on your back on the floor again. Because you are unique, with unique experiences, interests, and developed abilities, the answers

to the first four questions will be unique to you. Speaking in general terms, everyone is tasked with finding their own answers.

Now remember that there are two types of confidence. One is the general confidence that you place in your humanity. If one human being can do something, then every other human can do it also. If one human can run a sub-four-minute mile, others soon follow. If one human can do a headstand, then the rest of the species is capable of such things. More to the point, if one human being can answer these questions and make the answers meaningful in their life, then you can too. The first kind of confidence is confidence in the extremely complex human nervous system. You have all this ability at your disposal. Confidence is a choice. Spend a few minutes choosing to pursue this journey of asking with the knowledge and confidence that you, like everyone else, are more than able to find purpose, meaning, and satisfaction. Choose, work toward, and insist on a confident mindset as a foundation. Take a break, walk around for a bit, and then come back to where you were, and lie down on the floor again.

3. Now ask yourself two more questions:
    a. If I know what I want, what is stopping me from pursuing it?
    b. What is stopping me from developing myself to a high level in the areas I am most interested in, a level that would allow me to use my gifts to express myself and contribute to others by facilitating their learning?

    Stop right here, and take a few minutes to contemplate these questions. Take as much time as you need. These two questions could be a lesson unto their own. Answering these questions lets you know where the obstacles are and how to take action. Pause and rest briefly after meditating on these two questions. Stand up and walk around for a few moments, then return to lying on the floor.

By asking these what-is-stopping-me questions, you will get into the details of how you actually do what you want to do. And you may discover and inquire in more detail about the following: what your greatest mental strengths are and what their corresponding weaknesses are, what your physical strengths and weaknesses are, what your gifts are, and in what ways you powerfully relate to other people and to the world.

4. You might also ask yourself these questions:
    a. What have I done that succeeded?
    b. What have I done that expressed myself and that was fun and perhaps produced enjoyment for others?
    c. And especially, what works for me and what doesn't?

Be sure to allow sufficient time to contemplate each of these questions. It will do little good to ask questions without giving time to hold them gently in contemplation and carefully notice your response to each of them.

• • •

Remember that there are two kinds of confidence: One is the beginning belief that you can do it, that you can live fully. The second is developed as you actually develop greater levels of skill. The only way to increase your confidence is to integrate these two kinds of confidence. Together they produce self-belief, belief in others, and true confidence.

This lesson is a beginning point. You will ask these questions time and again. Asking questions is always a beginning. In time, you may find that your experience has guided you to the answers to many of these questions. You may also find that it takes a lifetime to fully answer many of them.

CHAPTER 8

Obtaining the Prize in Modern Life

Remember that you are an aware athlete: an *athlein*, one who strives for a prize. When we discuss ability to focus, it's apparent that the prize depends on the context. The original word for athlete describes one who contends or wrestles, so we will start with the first most literal idea of an athletic prize. To be an *athlein*, we must have great wrestling skills. Obtaining the prize in any context is a matter of developing the skills to grasp, seize, and take the prize by overcoming that which would stop us and being successful in a context-driven environment, whether it's wrestling, running, football, or any other sport or aspect of life.

But what provides the motivation to rise to a challenge? In Section 1, I presented a symbol of the obstacles that face humanity, the dominance of the lion on the great plains of Africa. Man's original place in that environment was that of a victim of the mighty lion. But that place was transformed. The lion, the great shaper of humanity, was both an obstacle and an opportunity for us to grow. It was a source of fear that provided the impetus for humans to seek security and then solutions to the problems the lion posed. Would mankind have developed as it did without this kind of challenge?

In the primitive world, there is no lack of motivation. It is inherent in the environment. Motivation comes through challenges to what we want. The more important something is, the more motivation we have to succeed. The more immediate the need, the more impetus we have to act now and to act decisively. What is important to you, and how important is it? How immediate is your need to succeed? How deep does the need go? What are your deepest values? What is in your way right now? When something is really important, we approach it with the attitude that we will do whatever it takes to make the thing real. Do you have that attitude about something you want?

• • •

FEAR

Fear is a natural, self-protecting response. It is an uncomfortable feeling we get when we face something dangerous or threatening. The fear response may be present in real or imagined circumstances. We should not ignore fear. To ignore it when we stand before our lion would be foolish. We should acknowledge our fears and overcome them through the learning process. Remember, the learning process starts with finding security and then developing better tools, skills, and support systems as our experience grows. Thus, the process of overcoming fear is not a foolhardy leap but a time-consuming journey of learning. It is a process not of just stepping outside of our comfort zone, which we might do incrementally, but an expanding of our comfort zone, our zone of competence. What are your personal lions?

• • •

WRESTLE FOR THE PRIZE

Athletics provide a good backdrop and clear visual presentation of the principles of what it means to obtain that which we seek. In his book *Win Forever: Live, Work, and Play Like a Champion*, football coach Pete Carroll describes reading about legendary coach John Wooden's coaching philosophy. Carroll writes, "It took him sixteen years to figure it out, I told myself, but once he did he absolutely knew it. After that he rarely lost, and he went on to win ten of the next twelve national championships."[36] The words "he absolutely knew" mean that Wooden's philosophy about winning was something he had synthesized from his personal experience, something that had come from his trials and errors and something he knew the details of intimately. What Pete Carroll and John Wooden were talking about first was how to win as coaches of their respective sports. But what they found themselves involved in were the principles of optimal human performance. That is, they understood how to wrestle for the prize in any arena.

When you wrestle for a prize, experience and the development of new skills are everything. Experience *is* knowledge. Without experience and skill, there is no prize. And the way to develop the skills that life demands is to learn to be present in the moment, to bring all of yourself to the now with full attention to the inner, *not* outer, authority, and to do it with a sense of enjoyment.

In sports, it all comes down to practice. But, it's not about how long the team or individual practices. It's about the details, the quality of everything they do as measured by the environment of the sport. More importantly, it's the intrinsic focus and experience

---

36 Carroll, Pete with Yogi Roth and Kristoffer A. Garmin, *Win Forever: Live, Work, and Play Like a Champion,* Portfolio/Penguin (2001)

of each participant. In life, it comes down to awareness of and being in the present moment. It is the knowledge of what resources you have now, what opportunities the environment is presenting at this very instant, and how to use available opportunities and resources efficiently that is the ultimate skill, the ultimate life practice, the foundation of new experience, the way to wrestle for the prize.

· · ·

THE PRIZE IS DETERMINED BY THE CONTEXT

When primitive man first killed a lion with a spear, he accomplished an extraordinary and joyful thing, not because he had killed a lion but because he had unleashed some of the potential of the human nervous system and had redefined his place in the world. He faced and became equal to a challenge, a challenge that required inner and outer strength. He expanded his self-image, creative abilities, and gained a new sense of security and possibility. By doing all this, he and those who helped and learned from him became more complex beings. They created wonderful experiences and a life worth living through personal and cultural growth. They increased their inner confidence in being human as well as specific confidences developed by increasing their skills. They faced and set aside their fears and grew through experience.

No human accomplishment and no individual's improvement are accomplished passively. These things only occur through the active will to involve the whole self in the learning process and by practice. No doubt primitive man practiced with the spear and practiced against smaller game before tackling larger animals. There is also no doubt that primitive man developed practices to still their doubts and overcome fears. Without doing so, they would not have been able to initiate dangerous hunts. Everything we need to know about fitness and adapting to the environment is evident in a study of primitive man, but we need to update the context to make it relevant in the twenty-first century.

Remember that what we are really talking about—adaptation—is the potential of the human nervous system to produce optimal human experiences and optimal human performance that results in greater enjoyment of life even in the midst of difficulties. In sports, some coaches do not teach beyond the fundamentals and place too much emphasis on our inherent desire to win and be recognized. The most successful coaches are those who have discovered that success is based on process, not by accomplishing an immediate goal. They have learned that their purpose is to lead participants to long-term experiences that maximize individual potential to learn. They focus on this during every stage, including while coaching their athletes to master the basics of their sport. Great coaches teach individuals to learn to control their consciousness, to focus, to leave behind distractions, to spend their energies building confidence rather than tearing it down. This takes practice, practice, practice.

To that end, many forms of practice have been developed since mankind journeyed outward from the savanna. These practices were developed to bring about a higher degree of self-control and self-awareness. There are yoga and meditation practices that have existed for centuries: breath work, Hanna Somatics, the Alexander Technique, and the Feldenkrais Method. All are helpful to integrate mind and body. Today, we also have specialty coaches who teach fundamentals of swimming, dance, running, triathlon, and the martial arts among others. We have life coaches, psychotherapists, somatic psychotherapists, and the list goes on. All these practices and coaching specialties are designed to improve our experiences in life by helping us focus our attention on specific thoughts and actions.

Awareness is the ability to observe ourselves. It is what allows us to know what we are thinking, sensing, feeling. It helps us identify our tendencies, habits, and relationship to the environment we find ourselves in. With this ability, we can make fine distinctions and improvements in our movements, actions, and behavior, distinctions other animals are not capable of. Through awareness, we can know how closely aligned to our goals and aspirations we are. Awareness is the ability to focus by directing our attention to the activity at hand.

Unique human survival skills arise from the ability to be aware. Awareness is the essence of being human. Though the ability to be self-aware is inherent in all of us, we must practice and hone our skills if we are to apply them to maximum effect.

· · ·

FOCUS

Many years ago, I decided to take the U.S. Postal Service exam. It was a test of skill. The test at the time had two sections: an address comparison section and an address memory section. I knew I had to do well on the exam because many people took it. My study guide recommended that I relate a word or letter to each number from zero to nine so I would be able to quickly make a sentence or story out of each address I needed to remember. I had a few seconds to look at and memorize each address during the test.

I went far beyond that. I related a letter or word to every number from zero to ninety-nine. I wrote them on lines in a notebook and began to take time by myself to memorize them. I went slowly from line to line and then randomly thought of the number-word relationship. After using this method, I checked my memorization skills. Once I was satisfied with the system I'd created, I tested myself at faster and faster speeds until I recognized the associations instantly. On the second part of the test, I used the practice tests in the study guide over and over, timing myself with a stopwatch.

My goal was to score 100 percent in less than the time allowed for the actual test. I learned how to move my eyes and use my fingers to track each line. I set aside, until my practice time was satisfied, all other things that might have occupied my time. When the time came to take the test, I was so prepared that I wished it had been a little harder because that would have eliminated more of the competition.

Preparing for this test required maximum focus on my goal. But this has not always been my experience. While developing the ability to focus attention on the task at hand is one of the most essential skills in life, I can think of plenty of times when it seemed impossible to avoid distractions. Can you think of times when you have been especially focused and clear on what you needed to do and times when attention eluded you?

The environments of the twenty-first century are complex. Still, the most successful teachers and coaches have realized that the principles of learning and achieving are applicable far beyond the playing field and classroom. If life is a process of continual expansion and learning, then each of us can improve our relationships; physical, mental, and spiritual senses of balance; and the performance of anything that is important to us. But it all comes down to committing to a kind of practice that can be characterized as *immersion*. We must dive into the details of our pursuit. This is possible when we are highly motivated. Perhaps it is the motivation to care for a loved one or the motivation that comes from a deep sense of purpose within us.

The most basic definition of fitness—that of adaptation—takes us into all aspects of life and goes far beyond exercise into the job/ work environment, the environment composed of relationships, the environment composed of all things we do that matter to us. What contexts/environments do you want to improve your proficiency in, do more easily, contribute more to? Anything can be faced, studied, practiced, and improved. We can improve our behavior in anything when we cultivate our powers of observation and focus and when we are completely and happily occupied with the task at hand. When we do these things, we are fully integrating tasks into our lives. But awareness would be of little value if we were unable to change our thoughts and behavior.

CHAPTER 8 LESSON:
MIND-BODY FOCUS

The first step when focusing the mind is to still the mind, to rest momentarily from conscious thought. As Mahatma Gandhi said, "Your beliefs become your thoughts, your thoughts your words, your words your actions, your actions your habits, your habits your values, your values your destiny."[37] Therefore, it is necessary to learn to control your thoughts.

· · ·

The ability to quiet the conscious mind is a powerful tool for improving life and a way to process things in the midst of turmoil because our ability to concentrate influences our success in life. By stilling the mind, we can find refuge from negative thinking, clutter, and worry. By learning to focus, we can also learn how to be single-minded and improve our approach to completing tasks.

I suggest doing Part 1 on one day and Part 2 and Part 3 on another day. Make sure you have a quiet time and a quiet room in which to practice.

· · ·

---

37 Gandhi, Mahatma, "Greatest Quotes of Mahatma Gandhi - My Life Is My Message", Heart Fables, March 23, 2015, https://www.youtube.com/watch?v=5jvdhGqvmLo

Part 1: Quiet Your Mind by Redirecting Your Attention

Take your time: Allow 15 minutes to complete this part of the lesson the first time you do it.

This part of the lesson can stand alone. You will do something different in Part 2. You may eventually wish to add a few minutes to this simple practice.

1. Sit comfortably on the floor. Or, if you are not comfortable sitting directly on the floor with your legs crossed, sit on a cushion. You may wish to lean your back against a wall, or you may wish to sit comfortably balanced in a chair. Either way, find a comfortable position before you start.

2. Focus your attention on an object you see in the room. If it is a small object such as a pen, you may hold it in your hand. Think about nothing else. Let the object become your whole world. Breathe with deep, easy breaths. Feel the life-giving air come in and the cleansing out-breath. Every time your thoughts wander, bring them back to the object. It is the conscious mind that holds all our worry and clutter. Focus on the object for only one minute at first. It is imperative to realize that your goal is not to perfectly hold your attention on the pen but to cultivate the ability to bring your attention back when it wanders. You may find your breathing becomes deeper, more relaxed as you let go of the urge toward conscious thought for a few moments.

Part 2: Cultivate Neutrality

Take your time: Allow 30 minutes to complete this part of the lesson.

In Part 1 you developed your ability to concentrate and narrow your focus. This time your attention will be diffused.

1. Sit or lie comfortably. This time, begin to observe yourself and your thoughts. Observe yourself as if you were standing off to the side observing a person who just happens to be you. Don't judge the thoughts you see as you sit calmly, and don't follow your thoughts anywhere. Simply observe what you sense in your body and what you are thinking. Each time you get distracted by or tempted to follow a train of thought, come back to the act of being an observer. Can you cultivate an attitude of neutrality? Can you observe without judgment? Can you empty yourself of distractions and remain open to whatever the present brings? Can you do this for 5 minutes, for 10, for 20? How might you carry this practice of neutral self-observation into your daily life?

2. If you remain a neutral observer without passing judgment, you will observe some thoughts that are at cross purposes to what you really want. In this lesson, you learn the practice of being an observer and may then be able to observe your habits, your fears, your desires, and your stresses. In this lesson, you will observe your alignment with what you want—what brings you into inner harmony and productive harmony with your environment—and be able to see where you aren't fully aligned with your dreams and abilities. In other words, in profound stillness, you can feel and discern what you really want and who you are and aspire to be. It is a process that unfolds.

3. Consider how you might become more aligned with your deepest desires.

4. Continue to observe yourself for several minutes. Cultivate a nonjudgmental, neutral attitude that allows you to be ready to move in any appropriate direction.

5. If you can observe yourself in different contexts, the quiet mind of the observer can begin to ask questions and let them be answered by something other than the ramblings and mullings of your conscious mind. Can you ask questions without passing judgment? It is possible to have your whole person available to answer questions such as What do I want? What should I do? How should I do it? If you listen with your mind and body, your whole person—the unconscious, the conscious—the mind and feelings of your body, then you can access the information you need to live with purpose and follow your dreams. When you observe an old pattern, a habit that does not express who you really want to be, how to take action will be clear to you. Remember, you are not changing your true self (though you may be substantially altering your current self-image). You are just removing some clutter.

Part 3: Observe While Moving

Take your time: Allow 30 minutes or more to complete this part of the lesson.

1. Go for a walk or an easy run. Find a place where you can move at a steady pace and without distraction. Can you begin to quiet your conscious mind like you did in the previous lesson? Perhaps you will simply quiet your mind as you move. This could be a goal in itself. To be able to quiet the mind after a day's work or activities is a gift. Or perhaps this time you want to hold a question in your mind. Can you observe the question? Can

you hold onto it without letting logic intervene to influence the direction of your train of thought? Can you let go of reason for a few moments and be satisfied with letting go? Can you let your subconscious mind speak? Can you let go of judgment and fear? Can you combine movement and quietness? How could stillness in action help you in life?

. . .

Stillness in action may at first be counterintuitive, but with practice, this powerful ability can help you reshape your reality. The conscious mind often uses up all the resources from which strength might otherwise flow. Everything can change when we get out of our own way. You may gain strength and a positive attitude when you temporarily let go of controlling the world and notice the beauty that is always present around you. You may find that as a result of this practice, you gain strength and a positive attitude.

CHAPTER 9

The Plastic Nervous System

From the earliest days, mankind has asked questions. Man has wanted to know what lies beyond the horizon, beyond what can be seen with the eyes. We ask: How do things work? Where does this new path lead? What can I learn by going on a journey? How can I take my journey inward? How can I alter myself and my environment to realize my dreams?

In a previous chapter, I introduced the idea of exploration, the discovering of new territory. Another word that bears examining is the word "adventure." To adventure is to engage in hazardous and exciting activity, especially exploring unknown territory.[38] Adventure takes the idea of exploration of the unknown a bit further; it connotes an activity that is exciting, an idea that makes us feel more alive. And it is in the context of adventure that we explore the exciting inner territory of the changeable, resilient, flexible brain.

The definition of "plastic" is the quality of being able to be made into different shapes.[39] Opposed to the idea of a fixed brain,

38 adventure, Dictionary.com, *Collins English Dictionary - Complete & Unabridged 10th Edition*, HarperCollins Publishers, http://www.dictionary.com/browse/adventure?s=t

39 plastic, Dictionary.com. *Dictionary.com Unabridged*. Random House, Inc., http://www.dictionary.com/browse/plastic?s=t

a plastic brain means the brain can continue to change through-out life. Today, the science of brain plasticity or neuroplasticity is cutting edge. Best-selling books like *The Brain That Changes Itself* by Norman Doidge have introduced the subject to the public.[40] But as recently as the 1990s, textbooks and mainstream educators still taught that the brain began an inevitable decline after a person reached maturity. The brain was thought incapable of producing new neurons. Advancing age brought on a steady, relentless decline in function. Intellectual life was on a downhill slide, and there was nothing that could be done to prevent it. For several hundred years, the scientific consensus was that the brain was a machine incapable of change once it had been formed. While it is easily observed that many organs in the body are capable of healing—the skin for exam-ple after a cut and even some of the internal organs have the ability to regenerate to some extent after an injury—the brain was thought incapable of healing. It is now known that the brain is an extremely adaptive and resilient organ. Thank goodness the pessimistic idea of an inflexible brain has finally been overturned. In contrast to the outdated understanding of the brain, science has now shown that the brain is capable of lifelong learning and can even change its physical structure to accommodate the learning of new skills.

What this means is that we are capable, at any age, of learning new and better ways of moving. We can improve our mobility into old age. We can improve even after an injury. We can do the things we enjoy longer. We can even add to our movement repertoires. We can change our habits to improve our health. We can improve our technique and skill when lifting heavier weights. Our self-image

---

40 Doidge, Norman. *The Brain That Changes Itself: Stories of Personal Triumph from the Frontiers of Brain Science.* Penguin Books, New York. 2007. 88, 197, 201, 204, 209.

can be changed. And we can improve in our chosen sports. Brain plasticity means that we can do all these things and more.

In 1989, Mark Allen, who had tried six times to win the Hawaii Ironman race, was in the final miles of the marathon still racing shoulder to shoulder with great Ironman champion Dave Scott. Both were on a world-record pace. Partway through the marathon, as Dave Scott relentlessly upped the pace, Mark was troubled with thoughts of never being able to win the race after all the years and all the training he had put in. Dave Scott was too strong. Allen might as well have given up: The race was stupid anyway. Then, in the midst of being pushed to his limits and feeling his energy wane, he had a vision of a shaman.

He saw the face of a man whose countenance was that of great peace yet great strength. The shaman's expression was one not often seen in the modern world. Most people wear an expression of busyness, uncertainty, or stress. This image was of a man Mark had not met but had seen in a magazine he had been mindlessly flipping through. Now in the midst of the heat of the lava fields, the image changed his thoughts. His mind quieted; he began to be thankful for the moment he was experiencing. Allen realized that he was privileged to be racing alongside one of the greats in his sport in what was unfolding as the greatest Ironman competition to date. Mark replaced his negative thinking, and his energy began to return. This was the turning point in the race and in Mark's career. He went on to claim six Ironman world titles by working with Huchiol shaman Brant Secunda and deepening his understanding of what had occurred that day. What happened to Mark was possible thanks to the wonderfully plastic human brain and nervous system.[41]

---

41 Secunda, Brant and Allen, Mark; *Fit Soul Fit Body*; Ben Bella Books, Dallas, Tx (2008), 9

The ability to change our minds, our thoughts, our feelings, our actions, and the ability of our brains to be reformed through directed attention unleashes greater possibilities than most of us think. These changes occur with moment-by-moment choices. Most of us underestimate the significance of our ability to make these choices. If attention is what guides our ability to change ourselves, then it is of paramount importance that the public know about this new science of neuroplasticity and its implications because, as Feldenkrais said, "If you know what you are doing, you can do what you want."[42]

Our potential, our fitness, and our health benefit from neuroplasticity. While the human brain has always been plastic, the prevailing wisdom of past decades (that it was not) gave rise to a passive attitude toward change. Changing anything about ourselves and the way we do things is anything but a passive process. The brain is a grand learning engine, but nothing is learned without the choice to pay attention.

The brain learns by forming new neuronal connections, and it is legitimate to say that it is a use-it-or-lose-it brain. With directed attention, the brain is capable of learning, whether you are young or old. If a human has a problem, we can broadly say that the solution is to learn: learning new ways to adapt to our environment(s) and improve our health, even our mental health.

The good news extends to an injured brain, which we now understand to be quite resilient. Much new research shows that our brains are not only capable of forming new neuronal connections at any age but able to reorganize their whole structure if injured and that areas mainly concerned with one function can be used to do entirely different things so we can relearn and regain lost functions.

42 Feldenkrais, Moshe, Feldenkrais Guild of North America, (2017), https://feldenkrais.com

Strokes cause damage to the brain by disrupting the blood supply. Strokes occur in the brain not in the limbs.[43] And, in light of new knowledge about brain plasticity, emphasis in therapy should be shifted toward stimulation of the brain and nervous system through movement in order to help patients find ways to regain lost functions by reeducating their brains. The only limiting factors are the amount of undamaged cortical tissue, time, mental focus, and motivation available for rehab and regaining the lost function.

In Section 1, we saw that the ability to go on despite setbacks, operating in the presence of predators, and the necessity to learn new skills are prime examples of human fitness. Likewise, the ability to be resilient after a brain injury is a prime example of the use of brain plasticity and its application to modern life fitness.

Another area in which brain and nervous system plasticity is relevant is the idea of talent. "Talent" is a word associated with an old unit of measure. It eventually took on metaphorical meaning like it did in the biblical parable of the talents. Just like belief, talent has two meanings. Its first is what we associate with natural ability. Some people seem to have a genetic makeup well suited to perform

---

43 Researcher Edward Taub coined the phrase "learned non-use" to describe the paralysis developed after his infamous experiments with the Silver Springs monkeys. This term also applies to the paralysis developed in stroke victims. Taub developed something he called Constraint Induced Movement Therapy or CI in which he placed the patient's good limb in a mitt, making fine motor skill use of that hand impossible, and worked intensively with the affected limb for several hours a day getting the patient to use and expand the movement repertoire of that limb. Usually within two to three weeks, marked improvement was noted in the affected limb. Brain plasticity and the learning process were creating new functional connections in the brain. Taub, E. (2012), Parallels Between Use of Constraint-Induced Movement Therapy to Treat Neurological Motor Disorders and Amblyopia Training, Developmental Psychobiology, 54: 274–292. doi:10.1002/dev.20514. For more about learned non-use see Doidge, Norman, *The Brain That Changes Itself: Stories of Personal Triumph from the Frontiers of Brain Science*, Penguin Books, New York (2007), 197

a particular function. For example, they are taller than others and their physique may be well suited for basketball.

Some people, from an early age, seem to have an advantage when it comes to learning certain skills. The second meaning has to do with the long-term development of talent. But, research has shown that early signs of talent are not indicators of eventual success.[44] Going back to the biblical parable, talent is increased through use, not by sitting idly by with initial ability (potential). Talent is the result of focused attention, and focused attention happens when we are involved in something that interests us, something that gives us a sense of self-expression, something we are personally invested in.[45] In all these cases, the commonality is learning and the brain's magnificent ability to adapt. Talent is, therefore, an *expression* of what we are interested in and spend time focusing on and is another example of brain plasticity at work.

Understanding brain plasticity gives us the knowledge that virtually anything can be changed: Anything can be improved. Better yet, we can make changes at any age. If we choose, we can reverse or change lifelong patterns. It is never too late. The plastic brain opens up new worlds of possibility. Brain plasticity brings us back to the original meaning of fitness, that fitness is the ability to adapt to life's challenges.

Viktor Frankl, in *Man's Searching for Meaning*, relates that he saw men in concentration camps during WWII who had given up

---

44 Mumford, George and Jackson, Phil *The Mindful Athlete: Secrets to Pure Performance,* Parallax Press, Berkeley, California (2015), 128

45 Brain plasticity in adults is dependent upon having enough of a reward or punishment to motivate the person to pay attention throughout what otherwise might be a boring training session. If this condition is met then adult brains can change as much as those of infants. Michael Merzenich – see – Doidge, Norman; *The Brain That Changes Itself: Stories of Personal Triumph from the Frontiers of Brain Science,* Viking Press, New York, New York (2007), 88

hope: "Woe to him who saw no sense in his life, no aim, no purpose, no sense in carrying on. He was soon lost," and "What was really needed was a fundamental change in our attitude toward life. It did not really matter what we expected from life, but rather what life expected from us." Life ultimately requires that we take responsibility to find the answer to the problems we face and to fulfill the tasks that are constantly set for each of us.[46] In other words, taking or not taking responsibility is a matter of life and death or at least inner life and death. Everyone wants to be fulfilled.

• • •

At one time, I had a job that paid fairly well, but the hours were long and gave me little time to pursue the things I really wanted to do in life. I was living a life of futility. I suffered with the thought that I was wasting my life, working for nothing but to eat and work some more. I could not give up though. I had a wife who loved me. Bless her for being there during those days. I tried a number of things to find another path, more than once pursuing opportunities to be self-employed. I could never quite submit to my situation. I knew there was something else but strongly believed in doing everything myself. One day, I had a revelation, a softening of some of my rigid attitudes. Suddenly, I began to focus on investing in myself, being more accepting of the educational system, and getting help. With a small but profound change in habit, I went back to school. New doors opened. I made new friends. I got an opportunity to pursue further training in the things I was truly interested in. I am still on that path of growth and learning and, in a new way, discovering myself.

---

46 Frankl, Viktor E.; *Man's Search for Meaning*, Beacon Press, Boston (1959)

I shared my experience with having a knee injury, the result of poor movement coordination and habit. Getting help in this instance also "gave me my life back." Life is not a passive experience. It is something to be unraveled over time, something we seek to enter into, something that gets better with age. The ability to adapt, to learn, and to change is essential. But how much can we change? This is limited only by our commitment to the process.

The reality is that we don't want to change everything. If we changed everything, we would lose our identities. Our brain protects us from the instability that can be brought on by changes that threaten to destroy our inherent personalities and those things that express our authentic selves. But change can be good especially when we change habits that are not contributing to helping us live meaningful lives.

The oldest, deepest habits are the ones that are the most persistent, the most resistant to change. They *can* be changed, but changing those habits requires persistent mental focus and effort.

Pascaul-Leone likened repeated patterns to the tracks we would make if we spent an afternoon sledding down a hill. The first time we descended the hill, we would make a track. The second time, we would be more likely to take the path we had made the first time. When we stopped, some paths would be deeper than others. These paths represent good or bad habits, or, stated another way, habits that are currently useful or obsolete in our current situation. The more we take a path, the easier it gets to take that path. The paths can be modified, but the well-used ones take more effort to change.[47] That's how neuroplasticity works. When we do something

---

47 Doidge, Norman *The Brain That Changes Itself: Stories of Personal Triumph from the Frontiers of Brain Science;* Penguin Books, New York, New York; (2007) 209

for the first time, we find that it gets a little easier to do the thing the second time. Conversely, changing a habit becomes more difficult the more deeply ingrained the habit is. Neuroplasticity, free will or free choice, therefore, requires the work of consistent, applied focus toward forming new habits.

Neuro researcher Michael Moskowitz MD coined several acronyms based on the principals of neuroplasticity to explain the process of promoting change in the brain: *MIRROR* stands for Motivation, Intention, Relentlessness, Reliability, Opportunity, and Restoration. Moskowitz developed this acronym for his work with patients who experience chronic pain. It is also enlightening regarding the general process of initiating conscious change. Motivation has to be present. Intention—the idea here is to focus the mind in order to change the brain—must also be present. We must be Relentlessness, persisting moment by moment. We must demonstrate Reliability—a belief in the process of changing the brain, and take advantage of Opportunity by taking every challenge as a means of Restoring brain function and coming to a new normal.[48]

An important point about the will can be made. Using willpower is often thought of as forcing ourselves to do something. Yet the real use of willpower comes not through forcing ourselves but by eliminating the influence of competing thoughts through persistent, focused attention. Competing thoughts become less relevant as we replace them with a state of unified will (getting out of our own way) and *commitment* to the new idea. A world of possibilities is open to us when we step outside what's familiar and learn new skills. Yet, for the most part, we are wired to step out of our comfort zones only incrementally, improving the real us step by step as a lifelong process.

---

48 Doidge, Norman *The Brain's Way of Healing;* Penguin Books, New York, New York (2015)

OUR PLASTIC BRAINS AND FITNESS

If you doubt the need to include the brain in any definition of fitness, think of the emphasis Phil Jackson placed on mindfulness when he coached championship basketball teams. Think of Vince Lombardi's emphasis on the basics and the perfect timing and teamwork of the signature "Packer Sweep." Think of the skill of the ballroom dancer, the gymnast, the timing of the Olympic lifter, the accuracy of the pro quarterback's throws, the presence of the aikido master. What about the brain's part in making all the elements of a song or a painting coming together in complex unity? Think of the way that Muhammad Ali chose his strategy when he fought powerful puncher George Foreman, a man who could lift you clear off the floor with one of his punches, and the way George Foreman regained the heavyweight boxing title when he was in his mid-forties by learning from his mistakes and never again letting someone trick him into wasting his energy throwing punches that did not fully connect. None of these things are built on force or exercise alone. The most skilled among us have developed inner skills as well as outer. Think of the boxer One in a Million who, in the ring, turns his focus to the job at hand but later that day as a coach turns his focus to instruction: instruction using empathy, encouragement, and optimism. Later still, at home, he turns his attention to listening before speaking. This rare individual has learned the skill of situational awareness; he is flexible, adaptable, plastic.

The plastic brain supports the truly human qualities of abstract thought and awareness. The capabilities of the human brain to learn and change are what kept us alive on the savannas of old. These capabilities are indeed still the key to survival in the modern world. Believing in the human capacity to change is what gives us adaptability, mental and physical health, resiliency, and purpose. What patterns in your life have you found to be examples of old habits, habits learned in childhood? Old habits do not always serve the situations we find ourselves in today. But anything related to personal improvement can be changed.

As Dr. Feldenkrais said, "There is nothing in our behavior that is unchangeable except the belief that it is so."[49] Anything that we imagine, in terms of personal change, is possible for us. Any new learning—any new possibility that you imagine with focus, persistence, and with full commitment—can happen.

———————◆———————

49 Feldenkrais, Moshe, frequently attributed to

CHAPTER 9 LESSON:
BRAIN PLASTICITY

There is nothing in your behavior that is unchangeable. Let's look at one aspect of body image. It is possible for an accomplished athlete to feel depressed and even incompetent. In some cases, an outward aesthetic could be produced fairly quickly, but it is possible to sculpt a great outward aesthetic and still feel that something is lacking, that something has been left undone. How would a depressed state effect your body image? What does emotional health and even confidence have to do with the way you look, the way you interact with the world, and the way you feel? What does it do to your posture, your ease of movement, and your weight or sense of your weight?

In this lesson, I encourage you to sense and be attentive to the interaction of your emotions and your body and how they influence each another.

· · ·

Take your time: Allow 20 minutes to complete this lesson.

1. Lie on the floor, and try to reenact a depressed or anxious, fearful state or a feeling of incompetence. Choose a negative emotion or negative real-life experience you have had. Recreate that experience thoroughly in your mind, including all the feelings that went with it. Take the time to do and sense this state of affairs in your body. You might choose to reenact an experience in which you felt overwhelmed, unable to go on, a time when things were getting hard and you wanted to quit.

2. Now stand and walk around. After taking the time and expend-
    ing the energy to suffer by feeling confused or incompetent,
    what do you feel as you stand and walk around? What kind of
    posture and carriage do you have? How easy and free is your
    walking? How heavy or light on your feet do you feel? Do you
    feel strong? Capable?

3. Now lie on the floor and reenact an experience in which you
    had an optimistic and resilient state of mind. Feel connected
    to yourself and family and friends. Feel the joyful realization
    of your dreams. Take the time to feel this state of mind in your
    body. Play out a scenario in your mind in which you feel worth-
    while, capable, able to adapt and enjoy life. Sense your breath-
    ing, the support you feel from the floor, the level of tone in your
    jaw and throat. Sense the tone of the muscles in your face.

4. Now stand again. How is your standing different this time? How
    do you sense the weight on your feet now? Do you feel light or
    heavy? Can you move quickly now? Do you sense any difference
    in your feelings of strength? Can you see that all movement is
    connected to emotion?

• • •

Who you really are is more than the exercise you do, more than the
outward aesthetic that is a result of the choices you make. There is
nothing unchangeable about your behavior. You directed your attention to two states of being and noted the changes in the way you
felt, moved, and presented yourself to the world. Sometimes an old
habit encumbers us, and we find ourselves needing to learn something new. Brain plasticity opens up a world of possible changes.

CHAPTER 10

The Unity of Body and Mind, a More Radical Approach

Imagine a concept of body and mind powerful enough to let you do the things you most want. Two thousand years ago, the Greeks developed the idea of a sound mind in a sound body. They believed that for a person to be mentally acute, it was necessary and beneficial to exercise and keep the body in good condition and health. This is one view of mind-body unity. This idea, though, still contains a dualistic representation of humanity. But there is a more radical idea, the idea that the mind and body are inseparable.

. . .

TRUE INTELLIGENCE: EMBODYING THE THINGS WE WANT

What do we want? One of our most primitive desires and pleasures is our desire to eat: to be fed, to find fuel. We desire this for our inner life as well; it has the same need to be fed. It takes the whole brain and body to produce a satisfying experience. Human intelligence is more than intellect. It is the senses, the feelings, the movement, and the subconscious all present and applied to the challenge we're facing.

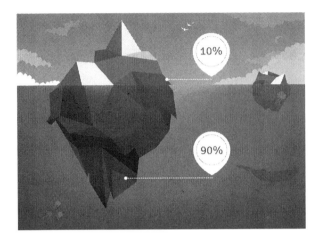

Figure 10.1. Iceberg intelligence—Balucius

• • •

A NEW CONCEPT OF INTELLIGENCE: MIND-BODY UNITY

Up to 90 percent of an iceberg may be unseen and found beneath the surface of the ocean (see Figure 10.1). Raise your right hand in front of your eyes and then set your hand down again. How did you do it? How did you accomplish the feat of raising your right hand? The answer can only be "I don't know."[50] Of course, some of you will try to answer with something like "The brain sends nerve

---

50 You might think that you know how the process of moving your arm works. You might say something about nerve impulses in the brain being directed toward the muscles in the arm. But you would only be using words to describe what you cannot feel or know. Which impulses? How many of them? How exactly do they connect? Can you feel any of this or keep track of all the connections mentally? If not, you do not really know how the arm lifts. Even the best instruments cannot keep track of all this.

impulses to the muscles, which causes them to contract." But which impulses? In which parts of the brain do they originate? How many of them are there? Can you sense and feel these connections? In reality, almost all our life processes go on below the surface. Almost all of them are a mystery and things we cannot directly observe. Although conscious activity is only a small part of the working of the brain-body, we almost exclusively identify it with intelligence and the brain. But what if we have gotten that wrong? What if there is much more to intelligence than just thinking?[51]

What if the body is where most of our intelligence resides?

We tend to separate emotions from rational thinking. We think in our heads and for the most part feel emotions in our bodies (and in a particular way in our torsos). Yet thinking without emotion lacks power, vitality, conviction, and life. Thinking without connecting with feeling may lead to wrong conclusions or actions, especially when it comes to relating to others. We separate ourselves from the environment when, in actuality, there is no separation. The environment is where we get all our information about what is going on in and around us. Emotions are, in fact, a complex chemical-thought relationship within the body and its nervous system. It is a relationship that is heavily dependent on the external environment. Instead of separating the two, we can think of emotions and thought as one intertwined process, the process of emotion-thought. Emotions are a kind of intelligence that has allowed the human race to survive. Bonding and societal structure were far superior survival tactics for humans than strict individuality, especially because human children require such a long period of nurturing. Altruism, the ability to

51 Wolkin, Jennifer, "Meet Your Second Brain: The Gut," Mindful, Foundation for a Mindful Society (August 14, 2015), http://www.mindful.org/meet-your-second-brain-the-gut/

connect to something greater than ourselves, is a kind of emotional intelligence. How humans make decisions is based on a thought-emotion process, and much of that is not purely logical and not conscious.

Conscious thought is only a subset of mind-body intelligence and depends heavily on language. Language is an extremely useful human invention, but most of what we know never comes to our conscious attention. The process we use to talk about a movement or verbally teach what we know about a movement is a different process than the process we use to actually do a movement. A verbal skill is not a movement skill, and a movement skill is not the ability to verbalize. We will never know how we move an arm. We also cannot know how our intuition tells us to avoid a person or situation. What we call intuition is a vast storehouse of information that we can't put words to.

We don't know how thinking without thinking (simply calling attention to a problem) can begin to organize what we know into a solution. How can we solve a problem by sleeping on it? How can we solve a problem when we take time to still the mind? How can we remember something that seems important or interesting simply by holding it lightly in attention and letting some subconscious processes work? We process more at any point than the conscious mind knows. The brain-body as a whole knows more than what the conscious mind is capable of knowing. Practical intelligence puts us more deeply in touch with the feelings of our body, including the organic feelings of anxiety, fear, confusion, resistance or acceptance, anger, joy, and the subconscious reordering of information we call intuition and the creative processes.

Brain plasticity explains how we can pursue fitness and self-improvement through our brain's inherent ability to change. But how do we change, utilize, and mobilize that of which we have no conscious awareness? The answer lies in the fact that all life is expressed in the body. All life is *embodied*. The parts of our self that escape conscious awareness are very much connected to how we express ourselves in the world. And the way we express ourselves is through movement. Let's take a look at the idea of embodiment.

. . .

MIND-BODY UNITY:
REAL-WORLD SKILLS AND BELIEFS EMBODIED

We develop real-world skills through experimentation, trial and error in our body and in our environments. The process of feeling the difference between one iteration and the next—feeling the difference between one result and the next—is how our skill at practical things improves. Sensing and feeling differences that we may not be able to fully explain is how we engage our potential.

Our conscious mind keeps us focused. Our emotions provide energy. The senses make distinctions.

Through the development of these real-world skills, our hands become calloused and our fingers more nimble. We project confidence both to ourselves and others through our posture. By taking up our full physical space and not folding and slouching, we move smoothly, easily, powerfully. We project engagement or kindness through our facial expressions, thought through the furrowing of our eyebrows, calmness or kindness through our smiles, and grace through our stride. Whatever we want in life will present itself through the full use of our mind-body. We learn to heal, to engage in new things, to persuade, all by immersing our minds and bodies as one in the experience.

A fascinating illustration of how we express ourselves through embodiment is found in the story of Baldassare Forestiere.

· · ·

AN EMBODIED LIFE FULLY LIVED

In 1906, an Italian immigrant arrived at the East Coast of the United States. He had been raised a farmer, and the young man in his mid-twenties had a problem. He owned no land in Italy. He thought that if he moved to the United States and worked hard, he could save enough money to buy some land and have the orchards of his dreams. In America, he made his living with his shovel by digging ditches. He eventually saved enough money to journey west to California. He looked for land in Orange County near Los Angeles, but the land prices were cost prohibitive. He needed to look further afield. He journeyed north and came to the Central Valley of California. There in Fresno, he was able to purchase 80 acres of land. Tragically, after purchasing, his inspection of the land revealed that it was worthless as farmland. He had purchased what he could afford. It turned out to be 80 acres of hardpan soil. It was so compact, he couldn't plow it, and it extended to a depth of more than 6 feet.

Baldassare continued to find work digging ditches and canals. He built himself a shack to get through his first winter in California.

The blistering summer heat of the Fresno area added to his misery. Temperatures in the area at that time could reach as much as 115 to 120 degrees. Baldassare decided to dig into the earth and build a little room in which to rest and get some relief from the heat. This room was so successful in helping him cope with the terrible heat that something happened. Baldassare began to think about building a habitation below ground, and then he began to wonder if fruit trees could grow there too. He experimented by planting a fruit tree onto which he'd grafted seven kinds of fruit. It turned out that the trees he planted in this underground area lived longer because they were protected from the summer heat and winter frost while still being exposed to sunlight from above. Baldassare's vision grew with each success. At one point he said, "The visions in my mind overwhelm me."

I have visited the underground gardens he left behind and feel that one cannot but be overwhelmed by the spirit and beauty of Baldassare's dreams. He used no power equipment and did almost all the work himself. It consumed his life and took 40 years of work and passion. What you see is not just underground rooms but a whole, embodied life, the beauty of one man's dreams. He had no formal education, yet he has been called a genius, a gifted architect who patterned his work after the catacombs of Rome—an artist, a designer. He employed the Venturi effect by mating larger rooms to narrower passages, thereby promoting air movement between rooms. He was respected in the valley as an expert at grafting fruit trees. He planned for a guest resort and excavated a ballroom. He even planned for the parking of automobiles by building a tunnel through which vehicles could pass.

Baldassare liked to say, "To make something with lots of money, that is easy. But to make something out of nothing, that now, is something!" Lorraine Forestiere, the wife of Baldassare's nephew

Ric, described Baldassare's legacy as a "testament to man's simple capacity to achieve with only the mind and body God has given us."[52]

The embodiment of his dreams would have been seen in his hands, calloused from forty years of digging. In fact, his dream was embodied in every cell of his body. Can you see how his self-image was evident in all his movements? Baldassare's story supports the basic ideas of what it is to be human; that is that a plastic human nervous system is capable of a great deal of adaptability, including the use of abstract thought to improve life. And an understanding of mind-body unity gives us tools to integrate our lives and do what we want, to use thought to produce better action, to use the body to make thought real.

Baldassare's story is not just about digging underground rooms but about making his personal visions reality. The concept of mind-body unity is the difference between a dream that remains a thought only and a dream that is acted on. To "enact" is to put something into practice. It makes all the difference between living the way we want and only wishing we could. All that we are in life, we experience in our body (the body includes the brain of course). With the idea that the mind and body are separate, we can think about something we want for all our lives but never be able to see it expressed. If we do away with the idea that the mind and body are separate and realize that we are a whole self, a unified mind-body, we begin to understand that it is possible to do and be what we want.

We find evidence for embodiment in the story of the great biblical strong man Samson and his struggles in life. To begin with, Samson had long hair that was an indicator of a commitment he

---

52 Forestiere Historical Center, Wilton, CA. (2006-2007), http://www.forestiere-historicalcenter.com/Forestierebio.html

had made to God. As the story unfolds, Samson became involved with a woman named Delilah who tricked him. As a result, his hair was cut off. His hair was a symbol of a chosen path and was, for him, a source of strength. When his hair was cut, his strength left him. Think of the shame he must have felt about unwillingly having his hair cut off and the weakness that followed, because everyone knew that Sampson's hair was a symbol of the way he chose to live. Eventually (in a slow process), Samson's hair grew long again. He regained his strength and faced his enemies. The story is symbolic but gives us a wonderful illustration of the power of the physical embodiment of our internal commitments.

When we think about the story of Sampson and how he became impotent, unable to use his full strength when his hair was cut, the role of muscles becomes more evident. Our bodies provide the senses by which we perceive the world, so we can regard our senses as part of our nervous system. We take in information through many sensations that we experience and form feelings about what we perceive. But there is another part of the nervous system we rarely think of as being part of the nervous system.

All action is expressed through movement. So, in essence, moving and acting are the same thing. No matter how much we perceive, we cannot express ourselves in the world without movement. And that brings us to our muscles. Without muscles, we cannot move. Therefore, we can regard the muscles as part of the nervous system.[53] This is not usually done because modern society is

---

53 Feldenkrais, Moshe, PhD. "Mind and Body," two lectures in *Systematics: The Journal of the Institute for the Comparative Study of History, Philosophy and the Sciences*, Vol. 2, No.1, June 1964, Reprinted in *Your Body Works*, Gerald Kogan (ed.). Berkeley: Transformations, (1980), http://www.feldenkraismethod.com/wp-content/uploads/2014/11/Mind-and-Body-Moshe-Feldenkrais.pdf

so conditioned to think of the brain and the body as separate from each other. But if we view the brain as part of the body, as science is beginning to do, we are free to think of the muscles in a more integrated way, connected to and part of the brain itself.[54]

With a newfound respect for the role of our muscles in terms of self-expression, it becomes easier to understand what Mabel Todd was talking about when, in *The Thinking Body*, she said, "We sit and walk as we think, [*sic*] watch any man as he walks down the avenue, and you can determine his status in life. With practice, a finer discernment will have him placed socially and economically, and with a fair idea of his outlook on life."[55] Todd's statement introduces us to the idea that our thinking is related to our sitting and walking; our thinking about our place in life is the same as the way we carry ourselves through life. Thus, all action is expressed through movement, and all movement is an embodiment of our thoughts, beliefs, emotions, history, and habits.

This suggests that if we change the way we think, our actions must change. Or, if we change the way we carry ourselves through life, our thinking and self-image must change. The idea that muscles are the effective part of the nervous system is also important because noticing the details of our muscular actions then becomes the basis of awareness. This is so because, as I pointed out in the example of the iceberg in the beginning of this chapter, most of our mental, emotional, and autonomic processes are unknown to us. Their workings lie below the surface of conscious thought. But when we

---

54 *The Comparative Study of History, Philosophy and the Sciences*, Vol. 2, No.1, 73 June 1964. Reprinted in *Your Body Works*, Gerald Kogan (ed.). Berkeley: Transformations, 1980. http://davidzemach-bersin.com/wp-content/uploads/2012/06/MF_Mind_and_Body.pdf

55 Todd, Mabel; *The Thinking Body; A Study of the Balancing Forces of Dynamic Man;* Princeton Book Co, Publishers, Hightstown, New Jersey (1937) Chapter 1.

express our existence by means of muscular action (an increased heartbeat, a change in our stance, a tightening of muscles, a change of expression), we become aware of them.[56]

The embodiment of life happens in one of two ways: incidentally or intentionally. So why not intentionally—by paying attention to our movement patterns—embody and create what we want? By using the power of embodiment, we can change the way we embody ourselves and create new patterns that are different from old habits.[57] It has been said that if you want anything in life, you have to work for it. But I'll add that if you want anything in life, you have to be willing to be transformed for it.

"Transformation" is defined as "a thorough or dramatic change in form or appearance, change, transfiguration, alteration, mutation, a metamorphosis during the life cycle of an animal."[58] Notice the idea of embodiment—the change in appearance necessary for transformation to occur. The body does what the brain thinks, and the brain thinks what the body does. As Dr. Feldenkrais stated, "Radical changes cannot be expected without reforming muscular and postural habits."[59] It was an eye opener when I discovered that the brain and body are inseparable. It makes such a difference in what is available in thought and reality. It makes a difference in

56 Feldenkrais, Moshe; *Awareness Through Movement*, Harper Collins Publishers, New York, New York (1972), 36th point number 7.

57 Feldenkrais, Moshe; *Awareness Through Movement*, Harper Paperback, Harper Collins, New York, New York (1972), 38. Feldenkrais puts forth the idea that our movement patterns are "hinges of habit" and, thus, the quickest way to personal improvement and that we can supplant or add to old habits through movement.

58 transformation, Dictionary.com, *Dictionary.com Unabridged*, Random House, Inc. http://www.dictionary.com/browse/transformation

59 Feldenkrais, Moshe: *Body and Mature Behavior, Frog* LTD and Somatic Resources, 830 Bancroft way, #112 Berkeley Calif, 94710 (1949) 218

what we perceive as possible and in where we place responsibility for thought *and* action.

It is useful to point out that breathing, which is a link to some of our involuntary autonomic functions, is also a muscular movement. Thus, the answer to how we mobilize and fully utilize the subconscious aspects of ourselves can be found in the muscles and in all the movements that comprise our experience of embodied living.

In fact, because all actions are embodied, and all habits depend on our motor patterns for expression, changing the way we move and portray ourselves through movement can be a powerful way to change a habit, which is the image of the movement itself and a direct path to improving adaptation and fitness and to personal progress.[60] In fact, when we change the muscular patterns upon which a habit depends, it is impossible not to be transformed.

Fitness is always about acting, and acting is always about movement. And movement comes about by way of the muscles. Becoming more fit involves becoming more aware of yourself and of your way of acting. Movement becomes the tool with which to do so.[61] Self-awareness improves movement, and careful observance of the way we move improves self-awareness.

———————◆———————

60 Feldenkrais, Moshe; *Awareness Through Movement* Harper Collins publishers 10 E 53rd Street, New York, NY 10022 (1972) pg. 38. He develops the idea of "hinges of habits" in pages 1-38.

61 Feldenkrais, Moshe; *Awareness Through Movement*, Collins, Publishers, New York, New York (1972) 36; Movement is the basis of awareness.

CHAPTER 10 LESSON:

USE THE WISDOM OF YOUR BODY TO CLARIFY THE UNKNOWN

What if you don't know what you really want? What if you need to resolve a conflict or a feeling that is unclear to you? If there is something you don't fully know or understand in your experience, then logic may not be enough. But there is subconscious wisdom that resides within our bodies, and this can be accessed by suspending logic and conscious thought and listening carefully to how the sensations in our body line up with words we can match these sensations to.

This is a powerful self-actualization practice you can use in many situations.

• • •

Take your time: Allow at least 30 minutes to complete this lesson. You may do more than one iteration, refining the process of finding a word to express (characterize) a feeling in your body: a "felt sense" of something.

1. Find a comfortable place free from distractions. Lie down and "scan" your body by noticing each part.
   a. What do you notice about how your body is making contact with the surface on which you are lying?
   b. Turn your attention to your legs. How do they feel? Are they heavy or relaxed: light, loose, or tight?

c. What about your arms and shoulders?

d. What level of tension do you feel in your face, your neck, your throat?

e. Turn your attention to your chest. Does your chest feel heavy, tight, wide, narrow, soft, hard? What is the feeling in your solar plexus?

f. How about your diaphragm? How do your gut, stomach, and abdomen feel?

2. Now think about what is troubling you or what is unclear to you. Maybe something is unclear about a direction you want to take in life. What is it that you really want? Alternatively, what is troubling you now? Do you know what that is; is it clear to you? When you ask these questions, do you notice any changes in the way your body feels?

Noticing the feelings in your body is a way to acknowledge the wisdom of your body and to ask it questions. The actual feelings in your body—your breathing, stomach, heart, etcetera—will show where your thinking does not match your bodily experience. Listening to your body in this manner will help you resolve and clarify many things.

Perhaps you are not quite sure what you want or are feeling uncertain about something. You may have a feeling of "stuckness." Do not try to figure out what you are feeling. Do not judge what you feel in your body. Do not go inside the problem or question it; just observe it. See if you can find a word or phrase that fits what you are feeling. Try out one word and then see if your body responds with something that indicates *Yes, that is it*, or *No, not quite*. Your body is a source of knowledge. Keep matching phrases with what you feel. You may have to repeat the process a number of times. You can use this process of matching a word or phrase to the actual feelings in your body anytime you need to clarify or resolve something that is troubling you.

For example, you might describe the way you feel with words such as *unclear, unsure, murky,* or *unsettled.* This is a first approximation, and you may feel some shift in the feelings of your body, some acknowledgment that you are on the right path. By acknowledging that this "felt sense" in the body is a lack of clarity, you can approach the process again by taking time to be with the feelings of murkiness. You can take another step (a second iteration) by trying to match another word or phrase to the new or clearer feeling. You might now match another word or phrase to this new feeling in the body that will clarify what you really want when you think about your goals. Perhaps the next word that matches what you feel will be *balance.* Perhaps something seems out of balance or out of place for you at the moment.

You may feel another shift in how your body feels as you come closer to clarifying what is troubling you. You may even now know where the lack of balance is. Let your body speak. Be patient; the process may take some time. When you have listened to the feelings and wisdom stored in your body and connected them to words and phrases that match, you may feel like a weight has been lifted off you.

• • •

Notice the feelings in your body now. Appreciate what has been revealed to you. Rest and allow some time to pass. You can return to this process again and again. If you make this a practice, you will eventually feel a shift toward clarity that will energize you. With more clarity, you will be able to proceed in a new direction in life and experience greater vitality.

If you would like to know more about how to use the wisdom of the body this way, you may be interested in reading *Focusing* by Eugene T. Gendlin PhD.

CHAPTER 11

A Change in the Brain Can Affect the Physical Structure

In the early part of the twentieth century, a young scientist, who was also an athlete, severely injured his knee while playing soccer. His knee turned laterally at a grotesque angle. The ligaments were lost and meniscus badly damaged. His knee swelled and lost fitness, causing him great pain. Eventually, his knee became useless, unable to bear weight. As a result of the injury, his other leg worked overtime so he could get around. In those days, the surgical options we have today were not available. Those that were available did not guarantee a good outcome.

One day, the man slipped on a slick surface and injured the leg on which he had relied for months. Now he had two injured legs. Hopping home was a difficult task, and he had to climb two flights of stairs to get to his apartment. Tired, he lay down in bed, but his heart was heavy as he drifted off to sleep. He feared that he would no longer be able to walk, a pill that for a young athlete was hard to swallow.

But when he awoke, he made an amazing discovery. The knee he had destroyed playing soccer, the one that had refused to support his weight for months, could not only support his weight but was now almost pain-free. He could still get around his apartment that morning. He was overwhelmed by his discovery and questioned how this was possible.

In his suffering, at a low point in his life, he had an experience that had a profound impact on him. His nervous system had reorganized his movements in a way that allowed him to get around fairly well with two damaged knees. He realized that if this could happen without conscious attention, he could study how this reorganization that the nervous system was capable of might be accessed with conscious attention. "At the time of the injuries, it seemed to me a wild idea to even consider it possible to effect a change in an anatomical structure through an alteration in the functioning of the brain, which involves negligible energy, compared with one in the skeleton."[62] This experience so affected the man that he devoted the rest of his life to unraveling and explaining this mystery and utilizing his discoveries to help himself and others. The man was Dr. Moshe Feldenkrais, a pioneer in somatic (body) education, human awareness, and movement.

• • •

IDEAL ORGANIZATION

Here is the key to using brain plasticity to overcome limitations. It is the idea of a better self-organization or even "ideal" organization.

Feldenkrais practitioner and athlete Sharon Starika writes, "I have a deep passion for running and have been a competitive tri-athlete and runner for more than twenty years. I was introduced to

---

62 Feldenkrais, Moshe; *The Elusive Obvious;* Meta Publications, 3601 Caldwell Dr., Soquel, CA 95073 (1981).

the Feldenkrais Method twenty-nine years ago after a debilitating accident with a semi-truck. The accident resulted in nine surgeries on the left side of my body and doctors gave me little hope of ever running again. Through practicing the Feldenkrais Method, I was able to heal myself, run, and compete again. From my remarkable recovery, I found my passion for movement and realized that I wanted to teach others to move with greater ease, comfort, less pain, and to live fuller lives with movement. As my mentor and lifetime teacher Moshe Feldenkrais said, 'Movement is life.'"[63]

Feldenkrais discovered that a change in the brain or a change in the way we organize ourselves to do something can allow us to overcome limitations and injuries so we can continue to do what we want. Learning to change how we do something, to use a different pattern, to move more intelligently makes the difference. Three important ideas—brain plasticity, mind-body unity, and reorganizing movement in the brain to affect a change in a physical structure—work together. Now we can all learn to use movement to improve and to become more aware of ourselves, to gain actual skill in sensing ourselves, and to use our skeleton and muscles better. This allows us to overcome plateaus and limitations.

The definition of the word "limitation" is revealing. It comes from 1350–1400 Middle English *lymytacion* or the Latin *līmitātiōna*, meaning to enclose with boundaries.[64] The word implies that there is potential outside the boundary. It implies that we currently have access to less than our whole ability. Our limitation is in what our brain currently knows.

---

63 Sharon's Story http://sharonstarika.com/

64 limitations, Dictionary.com, *Dictionary.com Unabridged*, Random House, Inc. http://www.dictionary.com/browse/limitations

A new way of organizing ourselves to do something requires learning to differentiate one movement from another and one pattern from another. Learning requires experience (trial and error) and a more refined understanding of how we do things. Learning new *hows* is what progress is about.

When I was struggling with knee problems, a video analysis of my running revealed that I was overstriding. It revealed poor timing and a failure to realize, differentiate, and feel the fundamental differences between running and walking. Overstriding occurs when a runner's foot lands not under but in front of the knee or when the timing of the stride is such that full weight bearing on one foot occurs not under but in front of the hip. When a runner overstrides with the foot landing in front of the knee, they may also fully extend the knee joint and land on their heel rather than their forefoot or mid-foot. When this occurs, forces are transmitted through the straight leg that is extended in front of the runner's center of gravity, and the rounded heel surface makes for an unstable landing pad. This can be very hard on the knees. Of course, it is not just the position of the foot that is problematic but the entire movement pattern, including how the pelvis and spine are used. Learning to improve movement can eliminate problems and promote healing. Developing greater skill in doing what you want is the key to progress. Skill trumps force and mindless repetition.

I am much older now at sixty-seven than when I injured my knee when I was fifty years old, but I have no knee problems that stop me from enjoying running. This is because I am continually learning new connections in my body that make my favorite activity possible as I age. Even a little learning in the right direction can make a huge difference. Learning is a continual process throughout life, and I have found that continual physical improvement is within our grasp if we embrace the learning process.

A few years ago, I went to another coach and had another running video made. I had plantar fasciitis problems at the time. I discovered when I saw myself on video that there was more learning to do. Today, I run better for my current body than I did years ago. I have no foot problems and recently completed a 30-plus-mile hike in the Wind River Range while wearing on my feet only sandals I'd made from old tires.

Even though I am getting older, I can still do the things I enjoy and learn new things about how I do them. Life is a process. Enjoy the process. Don't limit yourself with old-age thinking. An improvement in how we do something creates a change in our physical structures. By removing the stress created by inefficient movement, we give our bodies a chance to heal because we are no longer creating unnatural stress. We can then use our skeletons, muscles, and joints in the way they evolved and are best suited for use.

But how do we learn how to reorganize a troubling movement pattern? We must learn to make fine distinctions, fine differentiations between one movement, sensation, or action and another.

• • •

LEARNING TAKES TIME

After the publication of *Born to Run* by Christopher McDougal, the compelling story of the Tarahumara Indians, running sandals, and what barefoot running did for the author, shoe companies began to make "barefoot" and minimal running shoes.[65] These shoes were popular for several years. But what does barefoot running or running in minimal shoes do?

It increases proprioception, which is the reception of stimuli produced within an organism. Because you can feel the ground and your feet and toes are freer to move, your brain now has much more information to work with. This is a very good thing; it creates a rich environment for learning. But many people did not take the time to learn or make adjustments; they put on the new shoes and continued to train like they always had and then got injured more easily. It takes time and attention to learn a new skill. How long does it take to get used to barefoot running or running in minimal shoes? I can't answer that because I think the answer is different for everyone depending on their background and other factors. I know it takes time to learn though.

When I returned to running after I broke my right ankle, I did so in very stout, motion-controlling shoes. After that, I kept finding that each time I switched to a shoe with less support, I felt better. Through a number of steps over the years, I switched to lighter and lighter shoes. I went on to experiment with racing flats, and finally, I made a pair of sandals from thin pieces of Vibram material and leather laces. These were pretty close to barefoot. It took me most of a summer to acclimate to them. But over the course of several months, I adapted and was able to do long runs while wearing them. I found that after a winter of snow when I did not wear them, I had to reacclimate to them. However, this time the process didn't take long.

---

65 McDougall, Christopher; *Born to Run: A Hidden Tribe, Superathletes, and the Greatest Race the World Has Never Seen*, Alfred A. Knopf, New York (2009)

I also experimented with barefoot running on sidewalks and pavement around my neighborhood. This also took time. I started by walking a little way and then adding distance the next time. I rested my feet on grassy patches and got used to the shape my feet formed naturally to deal with rough surfaces and the natural way I used my arches so I didn't land flatfooted on sharp rocks. I learned to maintain a posture that would allow me to shift weight to my other foot more quickly to avoid pressure put on my feet when I stepped on sharp pebbles.

One day, I found myself a mile away from home. Usually, I would run some or most of the way back. At that time, I could be barefoot on pavement for 2 miles and could increase my distance from there. The value of barefoot running for me, on top of being fun, was that I received information about how to run efficiently, information I could not have gotten without the input from the bottoms of my feet. You may think that you have to toughen your feet to run barefoot, but the most important part of the skill is learning. People were buying new shoes for a quick fix, ignoring the brain and then blaming the shoes when they didn't achieve the results they desired. They didn't get the results they wanted because they hadn't taken the time to reorganize their way of moving.

But you can learn how to reorganize your whole way of being so you can move differently or move into life differently. You can also learn that this reorganization makes all the difference in whether you can function as you wish or not. But how does this process of reorganization work?

What does every child have when she is born? She has a complex brain and nervous system. But the nervous system is not capable of directing any coordinated movement unless the nervous system has a way of learning to do so. When it does learn, the whole organism responds to the environment and begins to learn to coordinate movement accordingly. The environment includes gravity. How does the child learn by interacting with the environment and with gravity? How does a child learn to walk for instance? A child may imitate, but imitation is not enough. First there is a process, a process of exploration. The child learns all the requisite things before attempting to walk. This is a lengthy apprenticeship. The child learns to track things with her eyes, to track the movement of her own arms and hands, to move her hands to the all-important mouth, to reach out and grasp, to move from belly to back and back to belly, and to use her legs for mobility by pushing on the floor, and soon after that to crawl. All these skills take thousands of experiments and many trials that produce a few aha moments and many smiles along the way. The child is totally absorbed in the learning process for years. And when she has the foundational skills and begins to walk, what happens? She falls on her butt many times only to get up again using the feedback from the previous trial to improve.[66]

You can be immersed in the learning process too. If you have the focus to persist in the process and the knowledge of how much difference making fine distinctions makes, you can improve anything. Neuroresearcher Michael Merzenich states that "everything that you can see happen in a young brain can happen in an older brain."[67]

---

66 Feldenkrais Moshe, Lectures given in Cern, Switzerland. Paul Dorn (October 17, 2014), https://www.youtube.com/watch?v=SBypfdEuDO0 and https://www.youtube.com/watch?v=JaIvaU6XvCM and part 3 https://www.youtube.com/watch?v=ZYuW5hDDw4s and part 4 https://www.youtube.com/watch?v=yNfB0WOnu74

67 Merzenich, Michael et.al., "Brain Plasticity Based Therapeutics," Human Neuroscience (V8. 2014)

Learning is an amazing thing: We can only learn a new skill if our nervous system, our senses, act in conjunction with our environment. This is the original process of a child's learning. It is the process we follow when recovering from an injury or a stroke. And it is the process of learning when we desire to improve our performance. It is an intense apprenticeship to the environment through our senses. It requires *immersion* in the process. Too often people want a quick tip or a simple fix, but that does not go deep enough. Trial and error, breaking things down, sensing and feeling, and perceiving improvement are processes. They are processes that, if followed, are far more powerful than what we have been led to believe.

The process of learning is the process of physical reorganization. Both healing and developing skills depend on this process. It's about imagining; changing habitual patterns in the brain; and going through the experimental process, the process of learning how to do things differently and in an improved manner. These are the foundation on which we can build a new definition of fitness. This fitness is an extraordinary thing not because we can change something but because we refine and elevate our place in the environment. We feel the joy and power of what we can learn and do.

CHAPTER 11 LESSON:

MAKE FINE DISTINCTIONS

This lesson is the key to implementing the wonderful discoveries Dr. Feldenkrais made about maintaining and improving function throughout life.

• • •

Take your time: Allow 20–30 minutes to do this lesson. Pause between steps.

1. Lie on your back on a pad or carpeted floor. Notice your contact with the floor. Where are the places your body is not in contact with the floor, and where are the places more of your body is in contact with the floor? Do you have one side of your body that is overall more in contact with the floor than the other? If so, is that your right side or left?

2. Notice your breathing. Let your jaw relax and your teeth part a bit. Feel the air come in through your mouth and over your teeth.

3. Your lips have many sensory nerves. Feel the shape of your lips. Feel the weight of your lips as they lay on your teeth. Can you feel the gentle pressure that gravity is exerting to shape your lips over your teeth? Notice fine details. What is the difference between the shape of your lips on your right side as compared to your left? Open and close your lips slightly as if starting to

smile or frown. Notice how they are connected to your cheeks, eyes, and forehead.

4. Roll over and lie on the side you noticed has more contact with the floor. If you are lying on your left side, notice how gravity is affecting the two sides of your mouth differently. In this position, the left side of your mouth is being pulled slightly downward away from your face and toward the floor. Gravity is helping the lips on the right side of your mouth conform to the shape of your teeth. You may feel that the shape and sensation of the left side of your face is different from the right side. What does your tongue want to do? What is the sensation of air entering your throat? Does the passage of air create a different sensation on the left side of your throat than the right?

5. Roll back over onto your back. What is the contact of the two sides of your body with the floor now?

6. Slowly stand and walk around. Do you notice any difference between the two sides when you're walking?

. . .

Differentiation, the ability to notice the difference between one thing and another, is the key to reorganizing yourself to move differently in the world. The idea that a change in the brain can affect a change in an anatomical structure is how we move ahead. It is how you make your own discoveries because no one can tell you how to sense and feel and, therefore, how to make distinctions.

Reorganizing how you act comes through a prolonged process of personal exploration. The reward for this is being able to live the life you want and finding your way in the environment(s) in which you live.

Are you now better able to notice small differences? If so, you have made fine distinctions as you practiced this lesson, the kind of distinctions necessary for improvement. You can use this ability to make distinctions wherever they are needed.

CHAPTER 12

Exploration and Self-Fulfillment

Expansion, exploration, and adventuring (being driven to or enjoying the risk involved in venturing into the unknown) are inherent in the character of mankind. It is generally believed that modern man originated in Africa. History shows that the destiny of mankind was to expand into and inhabit every corner of Earth. According to archaeologists, there was a great migration of humanity that started in Africa and likely proceeded to the east toward India. This migration likely followed the seacoast where there were temperate climates and food available from the ocean. Evidence shows that humanity made its way from India toward Australia and New Guinea, something that would have required an ocean-going voyage of at least 45 miles. Mankind moved into the colder climates of Europe, and, finally, at least 15,000 years ago, into North and then South America. The great migration of humans into all the world was a process that took thousands of years.[68] It may have taken a thousand years or more to migrate from North America into all the South American con-

---

68 Gugliotta, Guy, "The Great Human Migration: Why Humans Left Their African Homeland 80,000 Years Ago to Colonize the World," Smithsonian Magazine (July 2008), http://www.smithsonianmag.com/history/the-great-human-migration-13561/?sessionguid=c4932ea9-a752-1aa9-062e-83999a5738a3&no-ist=&page=1

tinent. And then there were the great sea voyages of the Europeans and others who circumnavigated the globe.

The process of expansion continues to this day. Think of the grand adventure of the National Aeronautics and Space Association's (NASA) Apollo 8 mission. It teaches us much about humanity.

. . .

CONTINUED EXPLORATION PAST EARTH'S BOUNDARIES

In December of 1968, three men began the longest voyage in human history. The flight of Apollo 8 was only the second manned space flight of the Apollo program and was the first time humanity broke free from Earth's gravity and journeyed into space. Doing so required that they leave the relative safety found in close proximity to Earth. Taking almost three days from liftoff to lunar orbit, they bridged the 250,000-mile gap between the Earth and the Moon.[69] Their mission defined the words "new" and "first." They were the first to leave Earth's orbit, the first to see the sphere of the Earth as a whole, the first to orbit the Moon, the first to make a voyage to another celestial body and back to Earth, the first to see the Moon from 60 miles above its surface. The men who flew this mission took the iconic earthrise picture.

---

69 Smithsonian Air and Space Museum, "Man Around the Moon, Apollo 9: AS-503," National Air and Space Museum, Washington, DC., https://airandspace.si.edu/explore-and-learn/topics/apollo/apollo-program/orbital-missions/apollo8.cfm

Figure 12.1. Apollo 8—By Apollo 8 crewmember Bill Anders
(NASA [1]) [Public domain], via Wikimedia Commons

• • •

WHAT HISTORY TEACHES

It is evident that the history of our species is a history of expansion. It is a history of continual movement toward more and more complexity. It is a history of viewing setbacks and failures as challenges, unavoidable obstacles that offer opportunities for increasing our knowledge through learning. Nothing has stopped human expansion on Earth and now even beyond. Why is this, and what does this say about human nature or character?

• • •

WHY DO WE EXPLORE?

The environment always presents challenges, and humans have long sought purpose and personal and species advantage by pursuing and overcoming challenges. Challenge, adaptation, and the search for purpose and self-fulfillment are driving forces evident throughout history. They serve as landmarks of humanity's experience. What is it in the environment that motivates such responses by us?

Perhaps we should look at the question another way. We speak of mankind responding to challenges, but no one responds to challenges that hold no interest to them or that do not necessitate a reaction. The response comes from something that is inherent. Remember the famous quote from George Mallory who died while making his third attempt to summit Mt. Everest, the tallest mountain on Earth. When asked why he climbed Everest he said, "Because it is there."[70] But the mountain was not an obstacle to him when he was living in England. He didn't need to climb it for food, to escape from a predator, or to make his life more comfortable. The mountain created no necessary challenge for him at all. So, mankind learns through involvement with the environment. But it is not always the environment that creates the challenge. It is often our nature that creates the challenge, a nature that must expand, comprehend, and master. The mountain was only a challenge because it was a provocation to the human nervous system.

The answer to the question of why the human species explores is that there is something self-fulfilling in the process. The cheetah and the antelope might be satisfied to run at incredible speeds. The elephant might be satisfied with its awesome size and strength. The

---

70 New York Times, "Climbing Mount Everest Is Work for Supermen," The New York Times (March 18, 1923), http://graphics8.nytimes.com/packages/pdf/arts/mallory1923.pdf

lion and the wolf might be satisfied to hunt. The eagle might be satisfied to rule the skies. The mighty redwood tree might be satisfied to grow up toward the Sun. But humans are different. While humans have the same need as all other animals to eat, drink, and have offspring, these things are never enough to satisfy us. The reason is the mighty human nervous system. Humans have an even more complex inner environment than other animals, and that inner environment requires a different relationship with the outer environment. Humans must satisfy their sense of wonder. We wonder what is at the top of mountains. We wonder how it would feel to go there. The scaling of Everest is a good metaphor. Getting to the top of the highest mountain elevates our place in the environment. From there, we would have a new vantage point.

The human nervous system is inherently capable of making breakthroughs and doing new things. That is right, the human species is a breakthrough species. We cannot help ourselves. As the bird's wings are designed for flying, so the human brain and nervous system are designed for learning and change. Humans are always doing new things: exploring new territories, devising new methods of communication creating new technologies, and developing social structures and new ways to adapt to our environment. The ability to think in abstract terms and the power of awareness set mankind apart. Humans are more innovative, creative, artistic, and imaginative than any other animal.

What happens when you have a species that is so dependent on learning? You get a species that takes approximately two years to learn complex skills such as standing, walking, and beginning to learn to run. You get a species that takes two decades to reach maturity.

Four-footed animals don't need to master the complex balancing skills necessary for bipedal locomotion. This type of learning cannot be directed through imitation, but the cognitive and sensory motor skills required for human development must be developed through a self-directed process. No one can balance for you or teach you to do it. So, infants learn a skill and learn how to learn. This is being self-directed and self-aware: to literally and figuratively stand on our own two feet. We call this process self-directed, but we could also call it being autonomous.

Autonomous action is synonymous with the type of learning that is inherent in human nature. Fitness is about expressing inherent ability. For humans, that means taking advantage of all the direction, support, and knowledge available while—above all—becoming more and more self-directed. Like walking, self-fulfillment can only come through autonomous, inwardly directed learning. Humans can only be fulfilled when they have satisfied the needs of the nervous system to learn and to become more complex, to know and experience more, and to be able to pursue a purpose more fully.

But what if you already know a lot about what you are doing? There is always room for improvement. It has been said many times that Peyton Manning was the most prepared quarterback in football. He was known for continuously studying game films and for his focus on timing, cadence, and fundamentals.[71] He studied film into the wee hours of the morning, and he often caused defenses to stumble. You might think that after decades of playing football from his school days through a long NFL career, he would have learned enough. But that was not the case; he continued his habits of thorough preparation all the way through his last season. There were always more details to learn. And now Manning, who may not

---

71 Pompei, Dan, "Inside Manning," Sports on Earth, MLB Advanced Media, L.P. (2017), http://www.sportsonEarth.com/article/91281874/ to-understand-peyton-manning-one-has-to-know-where-he-came-from

have been the fastest or the strongest, will always be remembered as one of the greatest quarterbacks to play the game.

Self-exploration is crucial for improving in sport and, more importantly, in life, and essential to the process of exploration is the exploration of movement both mental and physical. Fitness is always about movement. Learning to be fit is learning the details of your sport, the details of your movement, the details of your mental movement, and becoming more precise when following a train of thought or the details of connecting with others. The exploration of movement is driven by the same thing that the exploration of the continents of the Earth was—a sense of curiosity.

It is not an occasional flash of curiosity that I refer to but persistent, moment-by-moment involvement in what we are doing. Exploration is very complex, very challenging. Fitness is developing your own particular gifts and inclinations. The most pleasant thing for a lion is to bask in the sunlight. The most fulfilling thing for a human is to bask in the innate confidence of the gift of humanness. That is our ability to adapt, to imagine, to explore, learn, and follow and be absorbed in purposeful and creative action.

CHAPTER 12 LESSON:

IMPROVE YOUR WALKING, HIKING, OR RUNNING ON UNEVEN SURFACES

In this chapter, I talked about exploration in a literal and metaphorical sense: mankind's great migration and the self-exploration we can do as individuals. The purpose of this lesson is to help you better explore on foot. Its deeper purpose is to explore the process of self-exploration that leads to self-improvement.

When we walk, we usually walk on smooth, level surfaces. Most of us work inside on floors designed to be level. Streets and walkways are not always level. Sometimes they have some slope, but they are usually designed to be hard and smooth. We live for the most part in an artificial world.

Nature is not like this. Nature gives us a constantly varied surface: soft, hard, steep, cambered, and uneven with obstacles and inclines. The realities of our environment demand constant adaptation. Our most natural movements—running and walking—involve the skilled use and movement of the pelvis. Smooth, level surfaces dull our awareness of some of the useful movements we could make. They teach us to walk the same way step after step in a way that is suitable only to the artificial world in which we mainly live.

There are three planes commonly used to describe human anatomy and human movement: the sagittal plane, which bisects us front to back (movement of swinging the arm straight forward and back occurs in this plane); the frontal plane, which bisects us left to right through our vertical centerline (movement in this plane occurs when the arms are raised to the side); and the transverse plane (movement in this plane occurs when an individual who is standing rotates their hips or shoulders forward or backward on a plane that is horizontal). The transverse plane is the only plane in which movement occurs in a horizontal plane.

It is normal for us to rotate our pelvis when walking or running and, if well-coordinated, the rotation helps lengthen our stride and decrease stress on our knees by keeping them pointed in the direction of travel. When we lengthen our stride, our pelvis moves in the sagittal and transverse planes.

In an artificially smooth environment, movement of our pelvis in the frontal plane is greatly reduced because it's not as necessary. Movement of the pelvis in all planes is essential to good locomotion. This lesson focuses on the frontal plane because it might be the most neglected during life and work where we are confined to smooth, level surfaces.

Let's do a movement lesson to clarify the value of moving the pelvis in the frontal plane. The parts of this lesson flow together, and it was designed to be done in one session.

• • •

Take your time: Allow 30–45 minutes to complete this lesson.

Part 1: Move Your Pelvis While Sitting in a Chair

1. Sit in a chair with no arms. Do not lean on the back of the chair. Let your arms be at your sides, not on your lap. Take time to sense and feel how you are sitting. Can you feel some tone in the muscles of your back? Draw your attention to the muscles of your lower back. Do they seem to be working hard to hold you up?

2. Now, draw attention to the muscles of your front side, your abdominals. What are they doing? Does it seem like your back muscles are working harder than the flexors of your trunk, the muscles on your front side? Do both sides feel balanced, working equally, creating a balanced, easy posture?

3. Draw attention to your sitting bones. Are you sitting a little behind them or a little in front? Intentionally rock between sitting behind your sitting bones and in front of them. Notice how your pelvis moves. This is movement of the pelvis in the sagittal plane.

4. Now, sit exactly on your sitting bones. This is a neutral position that's neither anteriorly nor posteriorly tilted.

5. Rotate your pelvis by bringing one side of it forward and the other backward allowing the knee on the side of your pelvis that is moving forward to move forward also. Notice that your low back is involved in doing this. If you are moving the left side of your pelvis forward, you may have to transfer some of the weight of your pelvis to the right side in order to make this movement easy. If you are moving the right side of your pelvis, you transfer some of your sitting weight to the left side. This is movement in the transverse (horizontal) plane.

6. Come back to the place where both knees are equal (where neither knee is out in front of the other) and your pelvis is not rotated forward or backward. You should be sitting exactly on your sitting bones in an easy, balanced posture. With both feet on the floor, can you slightly lift from the chair your right hip by shortening the right side of your torso and ribs and lengthening the other side, while keeping your head more or less in the center? This is movement of the pelvis in the frontal plane.

Part 2: Move Your Pelvis While Lying on Your Back

1. Lie on your back on the floor. Rest for a few moments, then shorten the right side of your torso/ribs. Make the distance between the top of your pelvis and shoulder decrease while lengthening the other side. You will draw your right leg up in relationship to your left: The right leg shortens; the left leg lengthens.

2. While still lying on your back, try this on your left side shortening your left leg. Try alternating gently back and forth.

3. Rest.

Part 3: Move Your Pelvis While Lying on Your Side

1. Roll to your left side. Put a hand or pillow under your head. Shorten your right torso/ribs, and draw your leg up without bending your knee.

2. Alternately lengthen your right side by pushing your leg downward. (Remember to keep it straight.) Do all this gently. Sense how you do it. Avoid doing the movements forcefully because more force will decrease your ability to sense what you are doing and how you are doing it. This is, again, movement of the pelvis in the frontal plane. This time you do not have the restriction of the chair. Can you feel the relationship between your legs and pelvis and your torso? Can you understand how this can be useful when you go down stairs or climb steep, irregular surfaces or descend steep trails? Can you see how awareness of this movement can be dulled or lost when walking on level surfaces?

3. Roll to your right side, and repeat the movements of lengthening and shortening your top leg.

4. Rest on your back for a few moments.

5. Come to a standing position.

Part 4: Your Pelvis While Standing

1. Stand and place your left hand on a chair or counter for balance. Now, lift your right leg. Notice what happens in your left hip. Pay attention to the activation in your left hip. Notice that the left hip engages to hold the right hip level or possibly higher than itself.

    This is what happens when a runner has good form: the hips stay level, or the free hip rises slightly, in response to the activation of the standing hip. So, even when running on a level surface, there may be some movement of the pelvis in the frontal plane. If the free side of the pelvis, the side where the leg is being picked up off the ground, drops instead of staying level, then you are using ground forces poorly on your standing leg. Again, feel what happens in your standing hip to keep both hips parallel to the ground.

2. As you practice this movement, can you sense the possibilities for movement of the pelvis in the frontal plane? Can you see how there is a time to lengthen your leg and drop your pelvis a bit even on level ground? That time is not when you pick up your free leg but right at the end of the stride cycle when it is time to switch standing legs. When your free leg is about to become your standing leg, a subtle movement of your pelvis in the frontal plane can be useful. Likewise, on uneven ground, especially steep ground, moving your pelvis in the frontal plane can take stress off your knees and make moving easier. Can you

see how rolling your pelvis in the frontal plane can help even out the rolling terrain you might hike or run on?

How much should you move your pelvis in the frontal plane? The answer is that it depends on the terrain you are on, your structure, and your ability to sense timing and differences. There is no one answer: It depends on your needs at the time. Experimentation is a valuable part of this exploration. It is only important to realize that all these movements of the pelvis—in the frontal, sagittal, and transverse planes—exist and can be used to improve running, walking, and other activities.

• • •

The movements in this lesson may seem to be about the pelvis, but they are about more than that. You can use this lesson to learn more about the process of living and your ability to continually improve how you do what you do and how you experience life. In order to explore the world, we must explore ourselves, our movement both physical and mental. Self-exploration leads to better movement in the world, both physically as we traverse distances on the Earth and metaphorically as we move forward in life.

SECTION 3

REDEFINING FITNESS

CHAPTER 13

The Beginner's Mind

This section will redefine fitness. But to get started requires a starting place. And that starting place is complexity. Why complexity? Because oversimplification is dangerous. There are many questions to ask and much to learn. But oversimplification, and oversimplification of what is involved in movement, is an assumption of the opposite: that there is not much to learn. This attitude shuts the door on progress. We cannot redefine fitness if we do not appreciate complexity. For instance, have you ever heard anyone say that walking or running is the simplest thing in the world and that all you have to do is put one foot in front of the other? While there is some truth in that, if you take this statement too literally, you will miss the experience of sensing, feeling, and improving your form. Failing to realize how much there is to learn is dangerous. Nassim Taleb sums up the point well: "Any reduction of the world around us can have explosive consequences since it rules out some sources of uncertainty; it drives us to a misunderstanding of the fabric of the world."[72]

. . .

72 Taleb, Nassim Nicholas; *The Black Swan*; Random House Trade Paperbacks, (2010), 16

THE DANGER OF REDUCING INFINITE COMPLEXITY TO A SIMPLISTIC PARADIGM

The human nervous system is the most complex on the planet. The human brain has one hundred billion neurons with several hundred trillion synaptic connections.

In the book *Go Wild*, John Ratney MD and Richard Manning refer to British scientist Richard Wolpert who asks the question, "Why do we have a brain," and answers with "not so that we can think, but so that we can move." It seems that the more complex an animal's movements, the bigger its brain. Ratney and Manning tell us about the primitive sea squirt, a sea animal with a rudimentary nervous system. For part of its life, the sea squirt spends its time moving and looking for a home. When it finds what it is looking for, it anchors itself and does not move again for the rest of its life. The sea squirt no longer needs to move. Therefore, it no longer needs a nervous system. So, it eats its brain.[73]

• • •

SIMPLE OR COMPLEX: STATIC VERSUS MOVING

"Static" means not moving, and we can examine "static" to increase our understanding of movement. Consider the use of the word in two contexts. First, you might have a static attitude: a strong, unchangeable opinion about everything. You know a lot and are sure that you are right. Or you might have a more dynamic attitude that recognizes that there is far more to learn and that new learning may

73 Beilock, Sian, PhD, " How Humans Learn: Lessons from the Sea Squirt," Choke, Psychology Today (July 11, 2012) https://www.psychologytoday.com/blog/choke/201207/how-humans-learn-lessons-the-sea-squirt

very well modify what you currently know. This is how Einstein modified Newton's laws of motion and introduced unlimited complexity to the original, simple paradigm.

In the same way you consider movement, you can compare a static structure to a dynamic, biological, moving human to get an appreciation for the difference between the simple static realm and the complex realm of movement. Let's use static engineering as an example, a simple building or the simplest of bridges.

Figure 13.1. Span strength—Tennessee Photographer

Think of typical home construction that employs either dimensional lumber or engineered lumber as beams, known as joists, to support a floor. You can see in Figure 13.1 how a floor is typically supported by joists. Engineers know that the longer the span of the individual beams, the greater their strength must be in order to withstand the forces that are placed on a working floor. This is also the simplest design for bridges. If you want to bridge a small stream, you might take two beams or logs and span the stream. You may also build a bridge floor on top of the beams. There are engineering tables that tell us what dimensions of lumber are needed for a given span and what the distance between each joist should be. The more complicated the structure or the longer a bridge, the more engineering must be done to ensure its structural demands are met. But once a bridge is engineered and constructed, it must be used for the intended purpose. Without rebuilding, the uses are confined by its original design. Now consider a complex, moving, biological creature—a human.

Figure 13.2.

Figure 13.3. Photos by Lee Ann Forrester

Figure 13.2 shows a common movement taught in various settings from physical therapy to exercise classes to movement lessons. Notice that when in the original position on all fours, the configuration of a person's body resembles a simple bridge. The brain now has to coordinate the parts of the body to support this position so there is stability and no sag in the lower back, something that might compromise the back if the sag is excessive. Now imagine the transitions to the other positions. As you lift each limb, you radically change the engineering necessary to remain in the new position.

You changed the structural requirements by moving to a new position. Movement adds complexity, and your brain—unlike manmade, static structures—is capable of keeping up with the constantly changing requirements of movement. Now add the diagonal configuration and the complexity of changing which limb you're extending and the complexity of timing the transitions. If you were to do the movement of extending the limbs slowly enough, you would see that there are infinite configurations between the original position on all fours and the last position with two extremities fully extended. If this was a static human-engineered configuration, each possible position would require a separate set of engineering calculations. Consider that our brains are smart enough to regulate the movements and muscle tone so our backs can support weight while doing this movement, thus changing the engineering again, and that a human can move smoothly from these positions into any number of other positions. Are you starting to understand the complexity of the calculations our brains make on an unconscious level, and are you beginning to appreciate the adjustments that are constantly occurring to keep you balanced by using sensory feedback to keep you physically adjusted? No human engineer can keep up with this process, and no algorithm can match the complexity and calculate for all possible human movement, especially considering that this illustration provides only one example of all possible examples of human movement within time and space. However, the human nervous system is up to the task. Given enough time to learn, the nervous system can make the seemingly impossible possible.

Thus, it is essential to appreciate the depth and complexity of movement and not to trivialize what we deem as common movements, such as rising from sitting, walking, and running. Our amazing brain is capable of continually improving coordination, and there is enough room for a lifetime of improvement. Do you see how an appreciation for the complexity of movement and the complexity of life will keep you from ever thinking that you know it all? Complexity means there is ever and always more to learn. Complexity leads to what is known as a beginner's mind.

. . .

ABSOLUTES KEEP US FROM LEARNING

At every stage of learning, we must avoid absolutes. Shunryu Suzuki puts it this way: "In the beginner's mind there are many possibilities, but in the expert's, there are few."[74]

If I say I am doing a movement correctly, I leave no room for improvement. But, if I say I am doing a movement better, I am open to further progress. Again, it is a matter of attitude. Do you have an open mind—a beginner's mind—an acceptance of complexity and a desire to learn new things?

---

74 Suzuki, Shunryu, *Zen Mind, Beginners Mind*, Weatherhill, New York (1970) https://www.goodreads.com/author/quotes/62707.Shunryu_Suzuki

An open mind is the key to allowing new experiences, to moving past old or ineffective habits and beyond mindless exercise.

An important point is that things do not happen when we are passive. Like a key in a lock, a learning attitude allows us to proceed through active attention. We tend to think in simplistic terms, such as *I can do this* or *I can't do it* without realizing that our ability to learn provides alternatives when things don't work automatically anymore. If we're open to learning, we can take an incremental approach to learning and/or further refine what we are doing.

We make assumptions that we are not strong enough to do something, but exercise and strengthening our bodies are somewhat passive vehicles as far as the brain is concerned. This is why exercises alone cannot improve human movement: walking, running, or any other activity. It does not give the brain any new information; it simply repeats an old pattern for a certain number of repetitions. Exercise does not address the learning needs of our complex nervous system. This why we have hope. When repetition of the same patterns fails to produce results, our brain can figure out new ways of doing things.

Say you want to improve your rock climbing ability. You might choose to do certain exercises to augment your strength, but these alone will not improve your climbing ability. It is the time spent climbing that gives your brain the information it needs to improve, assuming you pay attention to all the possible ways to move as a climber. Whether you are conscious of it, you are always asking questions: How far out from the rock face do I hold myself for this? What is the timing of that? If you are injured from a repetitive use injury, it is your nervous system that has finally shut you down and said, It is time to try something new. How about this?

Life is full of questions. It is full of answers to those questions, but the answers beg more questions. We learn through questions, and, thus, we look off into the depth of the night sky and see the ever-expanding universe of possibilities. As Steven Handel points out, the right attitude unlocks these possibilities: "There's an important kind of wisdom in knowing what you don't know. Too often we fall into the delusion of thinking we know a lot more than we really do. This is commonly referred to as 'illusory superiority.' This can often make us stubborn in our beliefs and unwilling to accept new information. Ultimately, it stagnates our growth. Recognizing what you don't know actually puts you in a unique place of power. It can improve your choices in life, because it's an honest view of your knowledge and capabilities, as well as your ignorance and limitations."[75]

Once we don't know—once we are looking for more—the path is open to trial and error and innovation.

$$\cdot \ \cdot \ \cdot$$

EXPERIENCE AND LEARNING OVER MINDLESS EXERCISE, REPETITION, AND FORCE

The object of asking questions is to find new information, new answers. To master any skill requires learning as opposed to mere repetition. As T. Austin Sparks said, "Man never learns anything theoretically."[76] Man only learns through experience. We learn through feedback and trial and error, not exercise alone. As Moshe

---

75 Dunning, David and Justin Kruger, "Unskilled and Unaware of It: How Difficulties in Recognizing One's Own Incompetence Lead to Inflated Self-Assessments," Journal of Personality and Psychology (1999), Vol 77, No 96, 1121-1134.

76 Sparks, T Austin, *But Ye Are Come unto Mount Zion*, Austin Sparks Net (1969) Chapter 1, http://www.austin-sparks.net/english/books/003986.html

Feldenkrais liked to explain it, "We do not achieve ... by repetition, muscle exercising, or by increasing speed and force, but by widening and refining the cerebral control of the muscle range."[77]

A beginner's mind is a deliberate choice to bring yourself to an acceptance of how little you know no matter how much experience you think you have. It is the opposite of being a know-it-all.

· · ·

MY STORY OF NOT KNOWING IT ALL

In my forties and for about a decade, I lifted free weights regularly. My goal was to get stronger. The core of my program consisted of multi-joint barbell exercises: squats and especially dead lifts, overhead presses, barbell rows, and exercises that specifically target the biceps, triceps, lats, core, forearms, etcetera. I was much heavier and stronger in those days. I was also involved in jobs requiring physical labor, such as roofing and working as a letter carrier for the United States Post Office. One day, I fell off a roof and broke my ankle.

That night my lower leg bruised all the way up to the knee. I was in pain. It was going to be hard for me to make a living. It was a low point physically, emotionally, and financially. I had no health insurance and not much money. I had no choice but to show up for work on Monday. So, I put on an air cast and went back to work.

I applied myself and was determined to run again. Step by step, I did run again. I worked up to a walk-run cycle that allowed me to cover 20 miles. I felt the ankle had not healed well and eventually, after my work situation changed and I got health insurance and sick

---

77 Feldenkrais, Moshe, *The Potent Self*, Frog Books, 830 Bancroft Way #112, Berkley, CA 94710 (1985) foreword xxx

leave, I had it x-rayed and found that it was still broken but had a viable blood supply. I had a successful surgical repair that required a bone graft and two screws. The surgery had gone well, but my knee started giving me problems. This threatened my ability to work as a letter carrier and didn't allow me to run like I wanted.

An orthopedic surgeon ordered a knee x-ray and an MRI. He told me there was a degenerative process occurring in my knee and, therefore, not to run anymore. I knew nothing at that time about the power of awareness to improve the way I do things.

I was still young at fifty years old. I was determined. I could not accept the doctor's verdict. I was also desperate. Thoughts of amputation and a prosthesis entered my mind, thoughts I now know were foolish and off the mark, but I did not know what to do. All my exercise was to no avail. I needed answers. The big question for me was, Where can I find answers? I didn't have them but knew that more strength would not solve my problems. It had to be something else. The excellent surgeon who repaired my broken ankle told me that she didn't have the answers to my knee problems. However, she encouraged me to keep looking. "The answers are out there," she said.

This was my crisis of not knowing. Eventually I did find the answers. I found a physical therapist who was an ultra-runner and familiar with the Feldenkrais Method and the Alexander Technique.[78] He told me that if I absorbed the things he was trying to teach me, my knee would get better not worse each time I ran. He was right. I also remember him referring to the hip extension phase of running and saying, "Let it happen." This caused a major shift in my running and personality because my habit had been to rely on force, not flow. Now, over sixteen years later, I don't have those knee problems, and I have run farther than when I was much younger. Before I was

---

78 I am referring to Douglas Wisoff, radiantrunning.com

injured, I took running for granted. I didn't know that there was so much more to learn.

Now I must—and do—approach running entirely differently. I seek harmonious movement from head to toe. My running is gentler and more reliant on movement originating from my core. Because I, like most of us, have asymmetries in my body, I find that the learning process continues. There are always more questions to ask.

There are no answers unless there are first questions. Sometimes we don't ask. We ignore ourselves, our bodies, our pain. But finally, as C. S. Lewis stated, "Pain insists upon being attended to. God whispers to us in our pleasures, speaks in our consciences, but shouts in our pains. It is his megaphone to rouse a deaf world."[79] When you understand that life is complex, you know that you don't know all and then you are willing to ask questions and willing to learn.

· · ·

Not Knowing

I want to know because I fear not knowing.
It is not safe to lose my way.
I grow weaker and I fear
Death or suffering await.
There are no answers I can see.
I am at wits end.
I cannot do this, cannot find my way to safe and higher ground.
I look and yet don't see
The path that leads to where I need to be.
I grow weaker and I fear
There are no answers that I see.

79 Lewis, C.S., *The Problem of Pain; Samizdat*, University Press, Quebec, Canada (1940)

I simply do not know,
And now I am at the point of despair.
I need answers and they are nowhere.
I simply do not know.
I stop and see no way out.
This is a bleak dead end.
I thought I knew, but now I don't.
I look deep into the night sky
The blackness and the infinite stars
No one has known the depth of this universe.
Questions abound far more than answers.
Not knowing is greater than knowing by far.
Knowing is an illusion, shutting doors.
Questions, the hallway to the infinite library.
I accept the risk,
I say, "Here am I."
It is only through not knowing that I look further.
I look up and see from a higher vantage what I had missed,
And now my answers come one by one.
I see my way and I am saved.
Oh, frightening depth and blackness,
Oh, blessed process
That finally breaks forth with new knowledge, new hope,
I tread the corridors of the unknown carefully,
I respect the abyss.
Oh, frightful blessed process
For I am safe for the moment.
I rise up on new wings to heaven
Yet I am humbled.

. . .

MORE NOT KNOWING: HIKING IN THE DESERT

As Edward Yu says, "Even though not-knowing has a bad name in our culture, it is actually a gift that allows us to stand in wonder. Life in fact never really gets boring if you are willing to not know all the answers."[80]

Life is complex. It brings unexpected circumstances. It challenges us with what we do not know and then it gives us new insight. Sometimes we find ourselves in desert places. We may need to find our way like I did.

I tell the following story in present tense because I feel it gives a more immediate feeling to the experience:

I have been in the desert with my dog, Stealth, for two days. I am on my way from Walker Pass to Kennedy Meadows on the Pacific Crest Trail (the PCT) covering almost 20 miles a day. This morning I awoke expecting a slightly shorter day of hiking. But now, I have been moving quickly for five hours. I rationed water but don't have much left. I am in the high hills above the desert. It is May and already the temperature is rising.

The PCT is well marked. But, after five hours, I cannot find it. A gravel road goes to the right, and a gravel road goes to the left. Neither is the trail. I made good time going down one of the roads only to become fairly sure, after consulting my compass, that I was not going to find the trail that way. The way back is uphill, but I must retrace my steps. It is hot, and I am concerned. I have hiked the road to the right twice. Earlier, I passed a trail marker that seemed to indicate that I was going the correct direction. Clearly, I was not. I am now stopped under the shade of a tree after my second trip up the gravel road that

80 Yu, Edward; *The Art of Slowing Down: A Sense-able Approach to Running Faster*, Panenthea, Harrisburg, PA; (2001); 76

veers to the right of last night's campsite. I have exhausted my possibilities. I know I can't go without water forever. I am in a barren spot. I have trekked miles through a burn area. A fire from a season past turned the trees to sticks and charred carcasses.

I reflect on my sometimes-poor pathfinding skills. I doubt whether I belong out here without better navigation skills. I am at a dead end. I don't know what to do. I pull out my maps. The trail is there, but I don't see it. I begin to look for help outside myself. I look down at the part of the trail I have already covered. I don't see any other hikers. There had been one earlier. I am not sure where he went. There is no one nearby now. I say to myself I am ready for help from any source I can find. I look off in the distance and see what appears to be the trail in the place that it is supposed to be. But how do I get to it?

One more time, I head down the hill and come to the PCT marker, yet this is not the trail. And then, because I had seen something from up on the hill, I look across the gravel road to the right. There, in plain sight, is a rock cairn. I still do not see the trail but step past the cairn and then, I am on the trail again. Not only am I on the trail, but for a while it opens up wide and smooth and downhill. It continues downhill for miles although it gets rockier in places. I am excited, relieved. I shout to Stealth, "We found it. We are on the right trail."

Stealth's energy picks up. We are moving quickly and will make it to the next water source. We make it to our destination at Kennedy Meadows General Store shortly after dark. The journey takes on a different dimension. I found the way and hiked the path I intended. Next time, I will understand the PCT markers better. I now know there will be a next time.

Many times, our answers are close by, right under our noses, "the elusive obvious," yet we cannot see them.[81] Only when we stop to consider other possibilities do we find our way. More force or willpower is not the answer. I had already used willpower to hike rapidly. It had only gotten me lost. We often run into a crisis of not knowing. Sometimes this causes us to stop before we proceed in a better way. This is what happened to me in the desert. I came to a somewhat desperate place of not knowing. When this happens, we are at a dead end, but we know to question. In the next chapters, I share the way to find your answers—your answers from inside. We often do not have our answers simply because we don't first stop to ask enough questions. We don't ask questions because we think we already know the answers. Ask and you will learn.

In addition to needing answers for the knee problem I discussed earlier, I related that I had lifted weights for years. I enjoyed doing dead lifts and had progressed to a 400-pound lift for one rep on a couple of occasions. Yet years later at sixty-five years old and not having done dead lifts for years, I learned a nuance to the lift that I had not used before. By learning a different use and positioning of my hips, I was able to lift more than I expected and more than I could have without the new learned behavior. We can train our brain, not just our muscles, to achieve what training the muscles alone cannot. It is about not knowing. And not knowing leads to an open mind, which is the basis of learning.

We may exercise for years, but we do not realize that we are stuck in a habit, stuck in an old static attitude and have not been alert to new possibilities. We may hit plateaus that seem to signal the end of progress and growth. We persist in our efforts with willpower but don't develop new skills. In the end, we're disappointed

81 Feldenkrais, Moshe, *The Elusive Obvious,* Meta Publications. (1981)

or fall short of our potential. When we get to that place, life may open a new avenue of learning.

It is the brain that coordinates and improves movement. Training our muscles alone does nothing to improve skill. Many gains that appear to be strength gains are in fact neurological. The brain gets cleverer about timing, coordination, and muscle fiber recruitment. Train your brain to achieve your potential, not just your muscles. Exercise cannot make up for learning new skills; our ancestors on the savanna got plenty of exercise, but they survived by developing new tools, new skills.

By learning new skills, athletes have revolutionized their training. For example, athletes have made improvements in aerobic fitness by using the protocols of Dr. Phil Maffetone and training aerobically at very low heart rates.[82] By faithfully following these protocols for several months, athletes have found an initial need to slow their pace to maintain the required low heart rate. Eventually they have been able to run much faster without increasing their heart rate, which keeps them in the aerobic zone and burning fat. Thus, they have become much more efficient athletes.

And as Edward Yu says in *The Art of Slowing Down*, "This is to say that anything less than highly efficient movement, a powerful stride in the case of running, has little if anything to do with genetics, endurance, fitness, or willpower. It has everything to do with what we unwittingly do to block ourselves. Yes, you read it correctly: Our lack of power is our own doing, or, perhaps more aptly put, it is our undoing."[83]

---

82 Philmaffetone.com The Maffetone formula is a great way to establish an aerobic base by finding your maximum aerobic heart rate.

83 Yu, Edward; *The Art of Slowing Down: A Sense-able Approach to Running Faster*, Panenthea, Harrisburg, PA (2001)

Have you ever made a breakthrough or opened up a new direction in your life by learning something new? Do you know the value of not knowing as a starting place for new questions? Are you full of static attitudes? Or, do you appreciate and honor the complexity of life and the need for new experiences? If you have an open mind, you are ready to learn a new fitness paradigm.

CHAPTER 13 LESSON:

IT TAKES AN OPEN MIND TO LEARN

How often have you seen someone—young or old—performing activities of daily living such as walking or working out and noticed that their spine doesn't seem to move easily? If you haven't noticed, look around. The ability to flex, extend powerfully, and twist easily and gracefully is often greatly diminished especially in older adults. In my work, I often see older adults working out yet getting more rigid (less able to move fluidly) every year. A healthy spine should be able to flex and extend easily and powerfully. I see athletes with limited movement repertoires who lift heavy weights and don't know that their form is compromised. But we need not experience a downward trend in mobility or a life of limitations if we exercise our brain with our body. Along this line, let's do a movement lesson.

Be sure to move slowly through each movement. Take time to notice the effect of each as you do them. This will require an open mind because I will deliberately take you through familiar movements performed in many exercise programs. The object of this lesson is not exercise but to learn how to do these movements more efficiently and easily. Resist the urge to exercise during the lesson so you can learn the details of how you do what you do.

· · ·

Take your time: Allow 30–40 minutes to complete this lesson. Be sure to work through only one part at a time. This lesson can be completed in two sessions. However, if you have the time, it is better to complete it in one session.

Part 1: Fold Yourself and Activate Your Flexors

Lie on the floor with your legs stretched out and your arms by your sides. Notice your contact with the floor, such as points of contact and places where you are held up off the floor.

Lying on the floor reduces the muscular tension gravity exerts on us when we stand. Lying down reduces our effort when moving and creates a better environment in which to learn new patterns and observe ourselves. We can observe our postural habits. These habits are the same whether we're standing, sitting, or lying on the floor. The floor becomes a kinesthetic mirror. The more relaxed your muscles are, the more of you will contact floor. (You'll be wider and flatter.) Observe yourself. What is the overall shape of your points of contact? Don't try to change your contact. Is one side heavier than the other? Where are you the heaviest? How much of your body is in contact with the floor? What is the percentage?

Part 2: Lift Your Head with the Help of One Arm

1. Raise your head a bit from the floor a few times. Be aware of how this action feels. Raise your head and then put it all the way down on the floor each time. Relax your neck muscles between each movement. How easy is it? How high can you comfortably lift your head? When do you breathe? Can you feel your neck muscles working? Where in your neck do you feel the muscles working? Keep your effort minimal. Don't strain. Stay with very easy movements. Observe what the natural, effortless height you can lift your head to is.

2. Put your head down and rest.

3. Place your right hand behind your head to fully support it. Let your elbow hang toward the floor.

4. Now lift your head with the help of your right hand and arm. Does your elbow lift and begin to point to the ceiling as you lift your head? Is this easier than the first time? Notice that your head goes higher. Lift your head, several more times. Can you sense that as you lift your head your abdominal muscles are activated and that the higher your arm and head go, the more your abdominals engage? As you lift your head, do you feel some of your upper (thoracic) vertebrae rise off the floor? Notice what happens with your lower back.

5. Put your head and arm down. Pause and rest.

Part 3: Lift Your Head with Interlaced Hands

1. With the help of your arm, lift your head again. Was it easier this time? Are you more aware of your belly?

2. Put your head down, then lift your head with both of your hands interlaced behind your head. Your hands should be fully supporting your head. Lift your head as though you want to look at your feet. Keep moving: lift and lower, lift and lower. Do not leave your head up. Rest it on the floor between each movement. What does your pelvis do when you lift and lower your head? Does it roll backward on the floor to flatten your spine?

3. Lift your head again, and notice the work of your abdominals.

4. Put your head and hands down. Rest and notice any changes to your contact with the floor.

Part 4: Same-Side Elbow and Knee Together

1. Bend your knees, and place the soles of your feet flat on the floor.
    Place your feet about hip width apart, and balance your knees
    above your feet. Experiment with letting your knees go in and
    out to find the place where they are balanced above your feet.

2. Place your right hand behind your head. Keep your hand re-
    laxed. Raise your right knee over your chest, and take hold of
    your right knee with your left hand. Begin to bring your right
    knee and right elbow toward each. Do this many times. The
    object is not to touch your knee to your elbow. The goal is to
    feel how easy it is to move these two parts of your body toward
    each other. Remember, touching is not important. Leave room
    for improvement. Each time you bring your elbow toward your
    knee, aim it at a different place on your knee. As you do this
    movement again and again while aiming at different places, can
    you see how your ribs, head, and back organize themselves dif-
    ferently? Let your ribs be soft. Some people think of the ribs as a
    bony, inflexible cage. But this is inaccurate. The ribs are attached
    to the sternum with cartilage, and the ribs have moveable joints
    at the spine. If ribs were immovable bone, you would not be
    able to breathe properly. Therefore, we can say, "Let the ribs be
    soft. Picture and feel them as moveable, expandable, flexible."

3. Repeat the movement on your other side: Place your left hand
    behind your head, and raise your left knee over your chest. Take
    hold of your left knee with your right hand just below your
    kneecap. Now bring your left elbow toward your left knee and
    your left knee toward your left elbow. Repeat this movement a
    number of times. Aim your elbow at a different spot on your

knee each time. Put your arms and legs down and rest. Is your contact with the floor different now?

4.   Put your head down. Let your neck relax, and allow your head to roll a little to the left and the right. Let your legs be long, and rest with your arms at your sides.

Part 5: Diagonal Knee and Elbow Together

1.   Place your right hand behind your head. Raise your left knee over your chest. Place your left hand on your left knee just below your knee cap. Repeat many times the movement of bringing your knee and elbow together in this diagonal movement across your body. Notice how you breathe when you do this. Do you breathe out as you bring your elbow and knee together? Make sure the full weight of your head is on the floor for a few moments between each movement.

2.   Rest again with your arms and legs down.

3.   Place your left hand behind your head, and raise the right knee over your chest. Take hold of your right knee with your right

hand holding it just below your kneecap. Bring your right knee and left elbow toward each other gently a number of times. How is this diagonal movement different than the first one you explored?

4. Rest again with your arms and legs extended by your sides. Slowly roll your head from side to side about 2 inches.

Part 6: Lifted Head and Double-Knee Together

1. Interlace your hands behind your head. Let your elbows rest on the floor or close to the floor if that is more comfortable. Raise your elbows so they point to the ceiling and then bring them back to the floor a few times.

2. Breathe out as you raise your elbows to point toward the ceiling.

3. Pause and rest with your arms down by your sides.

4. Again, interlace your fingers behind your head, bend your knees, and bring your knees over your chest. Begin to exhale as you bring your elbows together, breathing out and lifting your head. Your arms are helping you lift your head, but notice the work of your abdominals. Bring your knees closer to your elbows as you lift your head. Repeat several times.

5. Lift your head and bring your elbows and knees a bit closer together. Put your head and feet on the ground between each movement.

6. Rest on the ground with your arms and legs stretched long.

7. Again, bring your knees over your chest, and interlace your hands behind your head.

8. Bring your knees and elbows as close to each other as you can while moving comfortably. They may touch, but it doesn't matter in the least if they do or do not. Do not strain. Stay in this position for a few moments. How much of your back and pelvis rise from the floor to allow you to bring your knees and elbows together? Pay careful attention to how much of your back and pelvis are still on the floor. What are the exact points of contact and support with the floor? Can you see how an awareness of these points of contact allows you to move more easily and powerfully?

9. With your knees and elbows still directed toward each other, gently rock just a little side to side.

10. Bring everything down to the floor and rest. What is your contact with the floor like now? Observe how the increased contact with the floor feels.

Part 7: Notice Differences

1. Lie on your back. Again, place your right hand behind your head, and bring your right knee over your chest. Grasp your right knee with your left hand. Now bring your elbow and knee toward one another. See how very, very easy this is now? Can you see how this movement of bringing your knee and elbow together—which is often used as an exercise movement—is actually very easy to do if you sense the parts of your body that press into the ground and the action of your hip joint, pelvis, spine, and shoulders? Can you see that your brain and coordination of movement are more important in improving trunk flexion than the effort that you put in?

2. Rest a final time with your legs long and arms by your side. Notice all the changes in your contact with the floor.

3. Taking your time, roll to one side and come to a standing position. Stand for a few moments and then walk around a bit. Enjoy your new feeling and organization while standing and walking.

. . .

By keeping an open mind, you have improved your self-organization from head to toe. You have learned to make flexing your trunk easy. You have learned step by step, part by part, how you do what you do and how to improve. You learned where and how to move and how to use your ground forces. You sensed the details of the parts and made whole-body improvements. In this lesson, you learned that movement in the spine does not have to deteriorate with age or injury. By paying attention, you saw improvements in your movement after spending only a short time doing this lesson. For example, what you may have previously seen as an exercise called a crunch has become an opportunity to notice how your body moves and how it can become more efficient. By slowing down and noticing, you can improve any of life's processes.

CHAPTER 14

Our Current Fitness Paradigm: The Old Fitness Pyramid

When we talk about an old fitness pyramid, an old fitness model, what do we mean by "old"? The word implies a number of things. Most importantly, it implies that there is nothing new going on. On an individual level, it implies that there is no new learning, no paradigm shifts, no new territory being explored. The Old Fitness Pyramid usually operates within the constraints of the definition of fitness as only physical fitness. As we saw in Chapter 1, fitness has an evolutionary origin.

Figure 14.1. The old fitness training pyramid

Fitness requires challenge and adaptation: survival. Fitness seeks to thrive and tends toward self-fulfillment. Fitness then is about living within the demands of a particular environment and meeting, and becoming more than equal to, those demands.

In the beginning, the hunter-gatherer lifestyle made certain demands. As mankind embraced agriculture, those demands changed. Cities emerged; societies became more complex. As time passed, organized, mandated group fitness programs were implemented by various societies to prepare the population for war if the need were to arise. This was true of the Greeks and Romans and many civilizations since. (Though it can be noted that both the Greeks and Romans were interested in aesthetics, the Greeks seemed to have had an understanding that exercise is needed for optimal health). Even the programs initiated in the United States by Presidents Eisenhower and Kennedy may have been more in response to Cold War pressures than for the promotion of fitness for the sake of the population's health. Even today some of our exercise programs are referred to as "boot camps," or we are said to be maintaining an exercise "regimen."

Many of today's fitness programs are based on a military model. The military model promotes the idea of training hard all the time with the idea of getting quick results since, of course, the first ninety days in the military are referred to as "boot camp." Quick results in the military context are justified because there is a need to quickly prepare recruits, mostly young people who by virtue of youth are somewhat physically resilient, for the physical and psychological rigors of war. Though this can be the expedient thing, it is only maintained for ninety days. Boot camps work! But there is much more involved in fitness than high-intensity training.

The boot-camp approach does not comprise an effective training program. It is a mistake in approach to train hard all the time. It is inefficient to maintain a high-intensity level long term without adequate rest, variability, and periods of rejuvenation.[84] Yet quick results are easy to sell to the public, so our concept of fitness takes a turn toward them. In the long run, there are no quick fixes. The military is not concerned with personal development during boot camp. The object is to bring everyone to a norm, a norm that might be far below the potential of some individuals but brings the whole group to some standard level. This makes the military approach a poor model for those who want lifelong health, to have individual goals or personal excellence, and are willing to take a long-term view toward utilizing more of their individual potential.

In the diagram of the Old Fitness Pyramid, the foundation is goal setting. We can call this a goal-oriented pyramid. The concept is very simple. You just set a goal for some external accomplishment and then begin following a training plan until you are injured, reach a plateau, burn out, lose interest, or accomplish the goal you set for yourself. A purely goal-oriented process is dangerous because it doesn't allow us to develop the patience necessary for long-term success.

The whole system operates on the quick-fix, quick-results mentality. This rudimentary pyramid is all most people have been taught. We can call it the good-enough pyramid, because it is good

---

84 The problem with physical progress is not usually that we don't push ourselves hard enough, but that we push too hard and try to meet expectations rather than carefully listen to the reality of what is. It is said that Roger Bannister, when he was training to run a sub-four-minute mile, had reached a plateau. He took a holiday to hike and climb in the mountains. When he came back to his training, he began to break through some barriers in his interval training, which led to him running a 3.59 mile. Scott Jurek—one of the most accomplished ultra-runners with seven Western States 100 titles, a Badwater ultramarathon winner, winner of the Copper Canyon Ultramarathon, and recently having set a new speed record on the Appalachian Trail—has been said to take several weeks off most years.

enough for a start, good enough for physical fitness, good enough for most things. If the goal is simple enough and easily obtained, the concepts in this pyramid may be enough. We use the simple steps illustrated in this pyramid every day. We may say, I want to walk to the grocery store that's two blocks away and get a food item. We then walk to the grocery store and return with what we went for. Mission accomplished; goal achieved. When you want quick results in something you already have sufficient skill in, this is a simple, organized approach.

When a simple goal is accomplished, it is because it is based on what we already know how to do. We may not have learned anything new after doing it, and it may not have tapped our potential or improved our life process. The Old Fitness Pyramid is based on using only the habits we already possess. When something more, something really significant, some big change is required, the Old Fitness Pyramid is not enough.

· · ·

ANALYZING THE OLD FITNESS PYRAMID

Figure 14.1. The Old Fitness Training Pyramid

When we break the Old Fitness Pyramid into three parts, it becomes easier to understand the positives as well as the inherent drawbacks of the pyramid. A positive feature of the pyramid is its simplicity. It is easy to understand, and everyone can and does use it at times. It has clear goal-setting and follows a plan: Sometimes people using it do achieve their goals. We all use this pyramid. In fact, most of our lives are based on this pyramid. But times come when we want to go further. We need something more.

When we want something beyond this basic idea—we need to learn a new skill, explore new territory, transcend a limitation, or pass from mediocrity to mastery—we are forced to look at this pyramid more closely. When we want something beyond what we have experienced before, our emphasis shifts, and we see this pyramid in a new light. Now the process section of the pyramid looks like what we see in the next diagram.

Figure 14.2. Old fitness pyramid gap

As you can see, this pyramid contains a process that is really not a process (Figure 14.2). When we want to explore new territory, the current fitness methodology (the Old Fitness Pyramid) becomes useless. There is no layer of learning. This pyramid simply tells you to go for it without giving you the means. If this is not clear to you, imagine a concrete wall that is 12 feet high and reinforced with steel. The wall has a deep foundation with steel rods penetrating all the way to bedrock. But the wall is only 12 feet in length. Would you really grit your teeth, get determined, and attempt to crash through the wall? Or would you choose to run a quick, clear path around either side of it? The first choice would surely lead to failure. Or we can compare the Old Fitness Pyramid process to a jump, a flying leap across the widest part of the Grand Canyon. Would you just psych yourself up, grit your teeth, and jump? Or would you follow a trail down and then up to the other side or find a bridge if one existed? One option is to tackle a challenge with brute force; the other is to be willing to learn by being aware of the situation.

Still not clear about the limitations of this pyramid? Don't worry. I will introduce a new fitness pyramid soon. In the meantime, notice that in this pyramid, there is no emphasis on self-awareness and no respect for the learning process or for developing individual ability and potential. As a result, we are left with an insurmountable gap, a foundation with no way to get to the top of the pyramid.

Tragically, many people fail to achieve their goals. You can exercise all your life and be met with great disappointment when you fail to achieve your potential. But there is a form of learning that is more concerned with *how* we do what we do than with *what* we are doing.

As Moshe Feldenkrais stated, "Formal teachings from childhood to adulthood seem to overlook the fact that there are ways of learning that lead to growth and maturity with practically no failures.

Formal teaching is more concerned with 'what' is taught than 'how'; its failures are very frequent."[85]

. . .

IMPASSE AND THE GAP IN THE FITNESS MODEL

A lack of self-exploration brings us at some point to an impasse, a complete halt to progress. It is time to stop attributing all our problems to a lack of exercise or a lack of strength. Please don't misunderstand, exercise has been shown to have a positive effect on every cell in the body, on the immune system, the muscles, bones, heart, mood, and self-image. But, I'm referring to the kind of exercise in which every repetition is the same and there is no exploration, no attempt to work with the brain to improve the quality of movement. We need a paradigm that takes into account the wonderful complexity of our biological being and the infinite variations of movements that are possible. It is time to think about lifelong physical and mental improvement and endless human potential.

As someone who has worked as a physical therapist assistant, I frequently saw patients who were injured not by work-related accidents but by their exercise habits. As a recreational runner, I have experienced what it is to deteriorate over time and the difference learning makes in restoring me to my potential, to a feeling of being younger or more capable. I have seen athletes who do not achieve their potential because they have not learned their fundamentals well. As a former letter carrier, I have seen the effects of repetitive movements over the course of years and how we need more awareness regarding how we do things in order to survive and thrive.

85 Feldenkrais, Moshe; *Body Awareness as Healing Therapy: The Case of Nora*; Frog Books, Berkley, California (1993); XIV

Again, as someone who has worked in the field of physical therapy, I have seen older adults participate in exercise programs at health clubs but get more stooped and less agile each year, and none of their training focused on how to minimize this through experience and learning. Much can be done about all this if we give ourselves time to learn and explore, thus filling in the parts left out of the Old Fitness Pyramid. Life doesn't have to be a downward spiral.

With the Old Fitness Pyramid approach, we always put in more effort. The New Fitness Pyramid approach is based on improving through a learning process. The real difference between the Old and New Fitness Pyramids is the difference between a life lived by old habits that, by the very nature of their constraint, forbid the continued growth necessary to utilize personal potential and live a life that embraces the process of expansion, exploration of new territory, and mastery.

CHAPTER 14 LESSON:
SAFELY EXTEND YOUR BACK

In this chapter, I said that the real difference between the Old Fitness Pyramid and the New Fitness Pyramid is whether you are operating by old habit only or exploring new options. You learned in the last lesson how to improve the flexion (bending) of your trunk. In this second lesson on improving the movement of your spine, you will have the opportunity to explore in detail how to improve your ability to use your ground forces and back muscles to extend your spine more easily and powerfully.

As you begin this lesson, do not feel that you must do all these movements. If you have shoulder or back pain, you may do fewer movements or visualize the movements that are difficult for you to do physically. You may also rest for a few moments anytime you want and then come back to the lesson.

· · ·

Take your time: Allow 30–40 minutes to go through this lesson the first time. Be sure to work through only one part at a time, pausing between each. Rest whenever you feel tired or find yourself straining.

Part 1: Hands in Push-up Position

1. Lie on your stomach. Place your hands comfortably above your head. How is your contact with the ground under your left shoulder, under your right shoulder, under either side of your

body? Notice what parts of your body are in contact with the floor. Generally, you will have more contact with the floor in this position.

2. Now, try to imagine which of your body parts participate in extending your back.

3. Put your hands in push-up position. Raise your head and look up. Do this gently a few times just to see how this movement feels. Use your hands only for support as you use your back muscles to raise yourself to look up.

4. Put your head down, and rest your hands above your head. What did you notice in your spine when you did this? Did all your vertebrae participate? Were there some that did not move much? Which ones? What part of your back moved easily, and what part did not move much at all? If one part of the back moves very little, then the adjacent parts must move more. This can lead to injury or difficulty in the parts that must overwork. So, let's see if we can involve more of your body, your entire spine.

Part 2: Lift Your Elbow

1. While still lying on your stomach, turn your head so you're looking right. Rest your left cheek on your right hand and your right hand on top of your left hand.

2. With your right arm glued to your cheek, lift both your hand and head together. Use light effort. Do you have a clear idea of which vertebrae are not involved in the movement? Make the movement easy. Make it about a 50 percent effort. Do this movement of lifting your head and arm several times. Then put your head and hand back down and rest.

3. Now switch to look to the left with your right cheek on the back of your left hand, and do the same lifting movement. Do only a few movements. Rest with your head down between each movement. Can you feel where in your back the muscles work to raise your elbow?

4. Put your head down and pause.

5. Switch again. Put your right hand on top and look to the right again. Now raise only your right elbow. Feel how high you can go toward the ceiling.

Part 3: Reach Forward and Lengthen Your Back

1. Put your right hand on top of your left hand. Your right cheek should be resting on the back of your right hand. Test how you are doing as you lift your right hand, head, and elbow. How is this movement now? Think of reaching and lengthening through your back as you lift. Just see if this idea of reaching out in an arc with your back helps you go farther.

2. Turn your head to the left. Lift your left elbow, hand, arm, and head. Notice if more vertebrae seem to be participating in the movement. What are your legs doing?

3. Lie on your back and rest.

4. While you are on your back, interlace your fingers behind your head. Let your elbows hang toward the floor. Bring your elbows together and lift your head just a little. Observe that as you lift your head and rock on your vertebrae, your lower back flattens. Do this movement a few times—very slowly and gently—just enough to notice what happens in your low back.

5. Lift your knees and your head and elbows. You don't have to lift high. Lift up a small amount, just enough to notice the part of your body that presses into the floor. Notice your contact with the floor.

Part 4: Notice the Contributions of Your Pelvis, Legs, and Spine

1. Roll onto your stomach again. Assume a push-up position. Put your forehead on the floor. Look under your body as you put your forehead on the floor, and feel what your back does to allow this movement.

2. Put your chin on the floor. Reach forward farther, extending your back when you put your chin on the floor.

3. Go back and forth between forehead and chin. What changes occur in your back and legs when you put your chin on the floor? Notice how important your legs and pelvis are to these movements.

4. Rest.

5. Place your right hand on top of your left hand with your left cheek on the back of your right hand. Lift your right arm and your head just to notice the weight. Lift your left leg only a

little, only a couple of inches, and notice what happens to your right shoulder. Do this several times. Lift your head, right shoulder, hand, and left leg together. Pause and lower them together.

6. Lift your head and right arm again, but don't lift your left leg this time. Slide your leg on the floor down and away from your upper body. Do you feel that your upper body is lighter? Does your upper body lift farther this way? Is more of your back involved than when you started? Is it easier to lift your arm and head and go higher? Do this movement a few times. Remember to always lower everything to the floor after each movement. You are moving in this lesson, not holding poses.

7. Place your left hand on top of your right hand. Turn your head to the left side. Imagine lifting your left elbow, hand, and head. Imagine a lengthening arc as your head comes off the floor. Now lift your head just a little—only a quarter of an inch—and notice what happens in your lower back and right buttock. Now lift your left arm and head and your right leg. Do your arm and leg feel lighter?

8. Put your head down and rest briefly.

9. Turn your head back to your right side with your right hand on top of your left hand. Imagine lifting both legs off the floor. Now reach and lengthen your legs, but don't lift them. Lift your head, right arm, and hand. Make only a few movements. Notice what happens with your arms and legs.

10. Put everything down, and pause for a few moments.

11. Put your hands in push-up position. Rest in this position. Look up toward the ceiling like you did at the beginning of the lesson.

Rely on your arms for support as little as possible. Do you go higher than at first? Now, bend your knees, and, once again, look up at the ceiling. Do you feel more powerful, more integrated in your movement? Do you feel where your pelvis presses into the floor? For some of you it will be easier to lift your head and extend your back with your knees bent and lifted. Others will find it easier to do with legs long.

Part 5: Relax Your Back

1. Roll to your back and rest. Do you have a clearer image of how your back moves and how your pelvis and back are connected?

2. Draw your knees together above your chest, and put a hand on each knee. Make large circles with your knees as if you were trying to draw a circle on the ceiling. Make the circles very round.

3. Reverse direction. Lift your head and watch the circles.

4. Stop and rest. Put your legs down.

5. Interlace your fingers behind your head, and draw your knees and elbows comfortably together a tiny amount. Stay there. Breathe comfortably and rock gently side to side. Rest on your back. Let your arms be by your sides and legs stretched long.

• • •

In this lesson, you used the muscles of your back extensively. You did some gentle movements involving the flexors of the trunk to relax the muscles of your back. Are the kinks ironed out? Rest and enjoy your contact with the floor for a couple of minutes. When you are ready, spend a couple of minutes walking and experiencing the new sensations in your back.

After you have done this entire lesson once, you may come back to it to practice segments you enjoyed and to increase your awareness of how to extend your back in harmony with the rest of your body.

This lesson is the New Fitness Pyramid approach in action. In just a few minutes, you improved your ability to extend your back and learned to do it in a safe and powerful way. To generalize what you have done, this learning is the process by which you proceed through personal impasse and improve your life—not through repetition alone but by increased understanding of how to do what you want.

CHAPTER 15

The New Fitness Pyramid: Learn First, Then Train

Figure 15.1. Douglas J. Klostermann www.dojoklo.com

How will you get past a personal impasse? It is time to fill in what's missing from the Old Fitness Pyramid. It is the learning process necessary when you want to go further than you ever have before. Learning how to do something through experience is what makes the seemingly impossible possible.

The Incas live in a land of impassable-looking canyons and high mountains, but through ingenious knowledge, experience, and co-operation, they live there quite well. In Figure 15.1 , where there was an uncrossable abyss, local people applied five-hundred-year-old knowledge handed down from the time of the Incan Empire to build a new grass bridge. It took only community effort, local materials, and three days to solve this problem. The Incas understood the process. Learning and experience bridged the gap, not trying harder or jumping farther.[86]

. . .

SUE'S STORY

Sue Billington tells a story that highlights her success with the Old Fitness Pyramid and the impasse she reached that required her to rethink everything. Sue, a competitive athlete based in Canada, found running easy. She loved it and ran every day. She didn't get injured, and she was naturally fast, having run times of 17:35 for a 5k on the track, 36 minutes for 10k, 1:21:00 in the half marathon and 3:08:00 in a trail marathon. The goal-oriented pyramid seemed to work fine for her. Set a goal. Train. Enjoy the results. But all that changed when she was involved in a head-on collision with a dump truck. Sue had gone as far as she could with the old paradigm. After the accident, she came to an impasse, an impassable canyon. She needed a new process to get to the other side.

---

86 Atlas Obscura, "The Last Incan Suspension Bridge Is Made Entirely of Grass and Woven by Hand," Slate (June 10, 2013), http://www.slate.com/blogs/atlas_obscura/2013/06/10/the_last_incan_suspension_bridge_is_made_entirely_of_grass_and_woven_by.html

Sue has no recollection of the accident. She relies on police reports to make sense of what happened. It took paramedics two hours to free her from the wreckage. Her excellent level of fitness is credited with helping her survive what could easily have been a fatal crash. Sue broke every bone in one foot, suffered a broken tibia and ankle, a collapsed lung, a broken rib, and a severe gash to her head. She was confined to a wheelchair for six months. Suddenly, everything was different for Sue. She was unable to do the movement that had come so naturally to her. It was no longer something she could take for granted. Sue now stood before the abyss, facing an unbridgeable gap. The old idea of just do it no longer worked. She didn't have the ability.

Today we look for an exercise prescription that will fix us, a pill from the doctor, a new supplement, or a few quick form tips. We turn to the experts. We want to be fixed. But we often don't turn our focus inward.

Sue sought help. "The compensations that I developed changed my gait and the pain in my foot created postural changes both in walking and running. I developed a limp, which was reinforced by my continuing to run with total unawareness. I developed back and hip pain and sought out treatments for these issues with sports medicine doctors, massage therapists, osteopaths, structural alignment specialists, Bowen therapists, and neuro-kinesiologists. These treatments, while beneficial in the very short term, were only a Band-Aid."

But early in her recovery, Sue realized something. She says, "I think the turning point for me was when I realized that I would have to fix myself using tools available with Feldenkrais and somatics, and stop relying on someone else to fix me."[87] Sue is a highly

---

87 E-mail interview with Sue Billington

motivated person who discovered that there is no substitute for sensorimotor awareness. Sue now has a greater respect for the learning
process and operates according to the New Fitness Pyramid.

Let's compare the two pyramids.

NEW FITNESS PYRAMID

Figure 15.2

OLD FITNESS PYRAMID

Figure 15.3

- Process oriented—long-term results
- Learning is involved
- Based on awareness
- Avoids success/failure paradigm
- Extensive experimental practice
- Personal exploration
- Innovation
- Very high levels of personal success
- Cultivating belief and confidence
- Learn at your own pace
- The master's pyramid

- Extrinsic goals—quick results
- Force over learning and patience
- No awareness—external directions
- Either success or failure
- Possible external goal achieved
- No experimentation—stick to plan
- No innovation—use existing habits
- Likely injury, plateau or setback, possibility of disappointing failure over the long term
- Learn at the group's pace
- The novice's pyramid

• • •

OVER THE BAR FOSBURY STYLE

The New Fitness Pyramid: Innovation a Key Difference

In sports, a great example of the difference between the two pyramids is the story of Dick Fosbury and the "Fosbury Flop." In 1968, most high jumpers were using scissors or front-roll techniques. They would approach the bar from the front and scissor both legs up and over, keeping their torso over their legs, or they'd approach the bar from the front and roll their body over the bar with their belly facing down toward the bar.

Figure 15.4. The Fosbury Flop—IPGGulenberg UK ltd.

A young high jumper who had worried that he might be the "worst high jumper at his high school and possibly in the state of Oregon," tried something different.[88] He went over the bar backward, landing on his neck and shoulders. Why did he do that? His coach had explained the techniques of the day, but when Dick strug-

88 Henry, Kris, "Fosbury Was No Flop," Mail Tribune (April 24, 2016) http://www.mailtribune.com/special/20160424/fosbury-was-no-flop

gled, his coach gave him the freedom to experiment. Fosbury began to have some success doing things differently. He is now known as one of the great innovators in sport. But at the time, his style was so unusual it was looked at as idiosyncratic, just something one odd guy did, and the term "Fosbury Flop" was coined.

Dick arrived at his technique through a natural process of awareness and sensorimotor feedback. He says, "I had the mental focus to succeed and then I just followed my body toward what worked." Dick made the 1968 Olympic team and represented the United States. He went on to win a gold medal but not before the German team told him that he was doing it wrong and could not succeed with his style. It turns out that the way Fosbury jumped has been shown to be a very efficient way to move one's center of gravity over a horizontal bar. We no longer remember the flop. We just call it high jumping because almost everyone does it the Fosbury way now. All this progress from one man paying attention to the minutest details of his movement. This is something beyond the grit-your-teeth-and-go-for-it novice approach. It is progress that cannot be attained from external direction. It requires and demonstrates the power of personal discovery.

• • •

AN EXAMPLE FROM THE WORLD OF MUSIC: INNOVATION THROUGH UNDERSTANDING

Laura Silverman is a gifted musician whose story is told in the book *The Mind and the Brain*. From the time she was six years old, she practiced the piano two hours a day, seven days a week. When she was eighteen, she decided to practice eight hours a day for an upcoming performance. Then one day she found that she could not play at all. She consulted with many specialists, including a hand doctor and a psychiatrist who told her the problem was all in her head. She tried acupuncture and the Alexander technique. Even botulinum toxin was suggested.

Then she went to another expert who gave her a diagnosis she had not heard before: focal hand dystonia. He told her there was nothing that could be done about the condition. But none of these experts were up to date on the latest research in neuroplasticity, the science of the brain's ability to learn and reorganize itself according to the demands of the user—to recover, adapt, and form new habits.

As it turns out, Laura's brain, due to intense, repetitive practice of movements that required all the fingers to hit the keys at once, had fused the images of the individual fingers into one entity instead of representations of individual fingers. The solution was to practice movements that helped her brain form an image of the individual fingers again. With intense focus and persistence, Laura returned to playing the piano.[89] No amount of stretching, exercise, or physical fitness could have given Laura her life back. (That is exactly the approach I have seen trainers take. They would simply have had her try harder to move her fingers and do a lot of stretching.) But there is another approach and an appreciation that the mind-body can recover like Laura's did. For Laura, simply trying to move her fingers was futile, but a clearer understanding of the neurological basis of the problem and a focus on involving her brain and sensory

89 Schwartz, Jeffrey, MD and Sharon Begley. *The Mind and the Brain: Neuroplasticity and the Power of Mental Force*, Harper Collins E-books, New York (2002) 201

systems—rather than trying, stretching, or forcing—put her on the path to improvement.

. . .

THE NEW FITNESS PYRAMID: MORE THAN PHYSICAL FITNESS

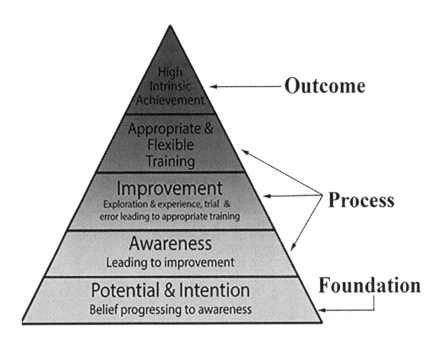

Figure 15.5. The new fitness paradigm

The New Fitness Pyramid is process oriented. The entire structure is based on learning. Therefore, it is not subject to a limited idea of physical fitness: It is about whole-person and life fitness. Fitness means fitness for your life, your survival, and the realization of your desires and dreams for yourself. As Mark Allen and Brant Secunda say in *Fit Soul Fit Body*, "We want to give you a different model of health and fitness, one that addresses not only your body, but the human being that is housed inside."[90]

Cultivating a love of movement can help you get beyond the concept of physical fitness as separate from mental fitness and position you for a lifelong program of good health through mind and body fitness.[91]

. . .

A UNIVERSAL ENTRY POINT

A drawback associated with the Old Fitness Pyramid is that it is based on repetitive exercise and often one-size-fits-all programs. These programs usually do not meet the needs of older adults in their sixties, seventies, and eighties. And they often do not meet the needs of raw beginners. Even so-called beginner programs often move too fast for the uninitiated. But because the New Fitness Pyramid is based on individual learning, it can provide an entry point for everyone. Consider that mental movement and physical movement are essentially the same.

Edward Yu explains the idea this way: "Learning intellectual and emotional skills follows the exact same pattern of acquisition as learning sensorimotor skills. In fact, the former is inextricably

---

90 Secunda, Brant and Allen, Mark; *Fit Body Fit Soul: 9 Keys to a Happier, Healthier You*; Ben Bella Books Inc., Dallas, TX (2008), 13.

91 Chang, Louise, MD. Reviewed by, "Mind and Body Fitness for Lifelong Good Health" Web MD, LLC (February 1, 2006) paragraph 2, http://www.webmd.com/fitness-exercise/features/mind-body-fitness-lifelong-good-health#1

linked with the latter to the degree that every intellectual and emotional state is simultaneously a neuromuscular state."[92]

With this idea, you can create an entry point into fitness. I first discussed the idea of an entry point when primitive man found respite from the fear of predators such as the lion in the stronghold of the cave home. That respite produced an environment in which they had the time to reflect, create, design, and build new and better tools and to incrementally improve their technology and skills. In keeping with our broader definition of fitness as self-fulfillment, something everyone is interested in, we need a universal entry point. Most exercise programs and fitness center staff do not focus on this universal entry point. Many people are put off by the lack of an environment where they can learn at their own pace when learning something new, something that's out of their comfort zone. Many people have also accumulated an assortment of injuries over the years, injuries that fitness instructors and center operators do not always take into account.

As I mentioned before, the universal entry point to learning is the imagination. To imagine a movement is the most foundational, most incremental starting point. Imagining a movement is the same as doing it.[93] From no ability to mastery, there is an incremental

---

92 Yu, Edward; *The Mass Psychology of Fittism: Fitness, Evolution and the First Two Laws of Thermodynamics,* Undocumented Worker Press, (2005)

93 Richardson, Alan, "Mental Practice: A Review and Discussion Part 1," Association For Health, Physical Education And Recreation, Research Quarterly, American (1967) Vol. 38 Iss. 1. In a study conducted by psychologist Alan Ricardson and documented in an article for Research Quarterly, *American Association For Health, Physical Education And Recreation,* published online March 2013, three groups of volunteers were tested to see how much they could improve their free-throw ability. The first group practiced shooting free throws every day for twenty days. The second and third groups practiced shooting free throws on the first day and the twentieth day. In addition, the third group spent 20 minutes per day visualizing making free throws. As expected, the second group did not improve at all. The first group improved significantly with 24 percent improvement. The

starting point for anyone when using the imagination. Emphasis on the use of imagination is something that is fundamentally lacking in most group exercise programs. So is the idea of self-exploration. If you can imagine a movement, you can begin to do it incrementally.

. . .

Dream big because you have more ability than you realize.

Notice that the new pyramid has a different shape overall and a different shape at the top than the first pyramid. This is because when we allow ourselves time and are committed to process-oriented learning, our intrinsic accomplishment can be much loftier, not limited by lack of time or the frustration caused by nonlinear learning. You can do virtually anything you commit yourself to. As Thomas Edison said, "If we did all the things we are capable of, we would literally astound ourselves."[94]

third group improved by 23 percent. Visualizing produced almost identical improvement when compared to physically practicing the movements. http://www.tandfonline.com/doi/pdf/10.1080/10671188.1967.10614808?needAccess=true

94 Edison, Thomas, "Innovate Like Edison," National Park Service, Department of the Interior, Washington DC (September 3, 2017), https://www.nps.gov/edis/learn/education/index.htm

CHAPTER 15 LESSON:

MORE SENSITIVE USE OF YOUR HANDS

The movements in this lesson may seem simple, but please remember that it is not the movements themselves that matter. What matters is how you direct your attention as you do them. This lesson will help you increase your sensitivity and better use your brain. These things lead to improvement in ways that mindless repetitions, stretching, and force cannot. Be sure to take your time.

• • •

Take your time: Allow 20–30 minutes to complete this lesson.

1. Sit comfortably in a chair at a desk. Rest your hands on the desktop and then carefully interlace the fingers of your hands. With your eyes closed, separate your hands, and interlace them again, this time doing it the nonhabitual way—that is with your other thumb and fingers on top. Can you feel the difference? Does one way feel more familiar? Unlace your fingers.

2. Now with your elbows resting on the desk, touch the thumb of your right hand to the thumb of your left hand, and explore the shape of your left thumb from base to tip. Explore all around your left thumb; feel its whole shape. Which thumb feels more sensitive? Rest with your hands on the desk, and feel the differences between your thumbs.

3. Hold your hands up again. Use your right index finger to touch the tip of your left index finger, then trace the whole shape of

your left index finger from its base to tip and on all sides. Gently explore the location of the joints. Feel the difference between the finger that is doing the tracing/exploring and the finger being traced. Explore and feel the space between your left index finger and the next finger, the middle finger on your left hand. Usually, the middle finger is the most sensitive of the fingers. Explore and feel this finger by touching it with the middle finger on your right hand. Examine it in as much detail as you did using your index fingers. Feel the shape on all sides. Feel the shape and location of its joints.

You must go slowly, and focus your attention on the sensation of tracing each finger in order to benefit from this lesson. This should take several minutes. Do the same sensitive exploration with your fourth fingers and little fingers.

4. Rest your hands palms down on the desk, and feel the difference between the sensations in your hands.

5. Open and close your left hand. Feel the clarity of movement in your fingers, joints, and hand. Do the same movements with your right hand. Notice the difference between your hands.

6. Rest your elbows on the desk. Close your eyes and bring the fingertips of each hand together. Starting with the tip of your right thumb, begin to explore the fingers of your right hand the way you did with your left hand. Again, take plenty of time to do this. Take at least a few minutes to do these explorations.

7. Rest and note the sensations in your right hand.

8. Close your eyes and touch your left eye with your left index finger. Can you feel the shape of your eyeball? Do the same thing with all the fingers of your left hand.

9. Repeat step eight by closing your eyes and touching the right eye with all the fingers of the right hand.

10. With your eyes closed, touch all the fingertips of both hands together, and make tiny circles at the fingertips.

11. Gradually interlace your fingers, then gradually interlace them the non-habitual way. Does this feel different than the first time you did this movement?

12. Come to a side-sitting position on the floor. With both knees bent and facing left and the sole of your left foot almost touching your right thigh, lean on your left hand. Raise your right hand toward the right side of your face a couple of times. Feel the support you have through your left arm and shoulder. What do you have to do in your left arm/shoulder to make lifting your right arm as easy as possible? Your breathing should not be affected when you lift your right arm, and you should not be distracted by an effort to hold yourself up.

13. Can you organize yourself well enough while side-sitting to maintain the sensitivity you developed in your right hand as you touch and feel the shape of your right eyeball? Do the same movements as you side-sit. Lean on your right hand to the right, and touch your left eyeball. Can you organize your whole self around the action of using your hand in a more sensitive manner?

. . .

I hope that after doing this movement lesson, you realize that you are capable of far more than you thought you were and how increasing your sensitivity can help as you explore all areas of your environment.

CHAPTER 16

The New Fitness Pyramid: Foundation

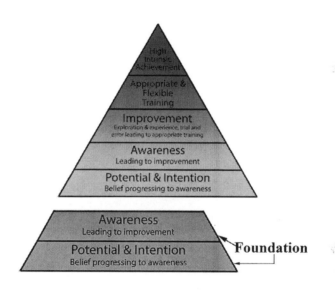

Figure 16.1. The foundation of the new pyramid of fitness

How can we explain and demonstrate potential? Actually, untapped ability is easily explained using the example of what physicists call potential energy. As I have said, potential is what is possible for you but has not been expressed. It's what you can do but have not yet done. The word "potential" is used often in the field of electrical engineering. It means that there is a difference in energy available (measured in voltage or electrical pressure) between two terminals of a battery. Energy exists and can be used. Energy can flow "downhill" from the high-energy source, but the potential is not used until the two terminals of the battery are connected in a circular path through a load. For instance, forming a circuit through the two terminals of a battery that must pass through a lightbulb gives us light. Light is evidence of potential and the use of the potential energy available.

However, there are two cases in which potential is not well used. The first is when there is an open circuit. An open circuit happens when a circular conductive path from the battery terminals does not exist or is not complete. In terms of human potential, this means that an intention does not exist. Once there is an intention in a particular direction, potential can be expressed. The amount of potential expressed depends not on the theoretically complete circuit but on the way the circuit is produced. To understand how potential works in real life, we must understand the concept of resistance.

In reality, all potential energy available cannot be used effectively. There is always some resistance involved. Your job as an engineer, an athlete, and ultimately as a human is to eliminate as much resistance as you can. You may be familiar with how electricity flows through copper wires. Copper is highly conductive. You could conceive of electrical wiring being done with steel wires. But in actual practice, steel wires are not used because copper is many times more conductive than steel. An electrical circuit designed with steel wires would not work effectively. Therefore, *how* you build the circuit is just as important as the *intention* to build it.

In order to reduce resistance and use potential more effectively, we must understand a few additional concepts. We must begin to understand factors influencing resistance and design: the comparative conductance of materials, the characteristics of the load, and the overall design intentions. In human terms, this means that potential is inherent. The actualization of it depends on designing a circuit or having an intention, and the living of it demands heightened awareness that leads to knowing and experiencing all the details of *how* to use our potential effectively. Potential and intention lead us to awareness.

To use a more human example of potential energy, let's consider high gravitational energy. Remember, energy flows downhill. Everyone has seen something fall from a high shelf or a rock fall from a high ledge. Humans have a high center of gravity when we stand. We store potential energy in our bodies like batteries do. It is as if a massive boulder were tenuously balanced on top of a high hill. Energy is available and can easily be released. This is a form of potential. Just as the energy in the boulder is held on top of the hill, the energy stored in our high center of gravity is held up by the bones of our skeleton. The narrow base of support for two-legged standing reflects the balance of the boulder. Humans are built for movement, not for static standing. Our narrow base of support and tall standing position make static standing virtually impossible. Stand up and stand still. If you are paying attention, you will notice that you cannot stand perfectly still. Pay attention and you will find muscles constantly making small adjustments to keep you upright. This seeming disadvantage is advantageous when it comes to moving however.

When energy in a battery is used up, the battery must be recharged. When a boulder topples down a hill and releases its stored energy, work must be done to place it back on top of the hill to restore its potential energy. The system defines the potential and the capacity. With humans, the system also defines our potential and capacity. Whether rock or human, once the vertical position has been lost, energy must be expended to regain it. Once in the vertical position though, it takes virtually no energy to initiate movement. The slightest thought about shifting the angle of our postural column forward and out of vertical alignment will initiate movement. It is a wonderful, even magical, discovery. Try it. Stand in what you feel is good but easy vertical alignment and then just think a thought about allowing your whole skeleton to shift forward at the ankles, and you will begin to move. Now we have in the human structure both an example of potential (potential energy) and the coupling of what is inherent with an intention (the intention to move).

Unlike the boulder that must be hoisted back to the top of the hill or the battery that must be recharged to restore potential, the human structure is much more complex and beautifully designed for upright walking. The perfect coordination of all twenty-six bones of the foot; the ankle; the knee; ball and socket of the hip; and movements of the pelvis, spine, arms, shoulders, and head make walking possible. And walking, when done skillfully, requires minimal energy to maintain. The human system can function quite well over long periods when used efficiently. Humans have been known to cover 200 or even 300 miles on foot with minimal rest.

Human potential then can be defined as the skilled used of the skeleton and skilled movement of the center of gravity. Deviation from the ideal use of the skeleton is less efficient (uses much more energy) and has the subjective feel of effort. Again, we can use the *potential* that is inherent (a high center of gravity), that which is inherent through *intention* (the decision to move), and heightened *awareness* to develop the skill to move well.

What do anthropologists and paleontologists study when they study human origins? It is the skeleton. The skeletal evidence defines what is human and what is not quite human. In the fossilized skeletons of our ancestors, we see the defining features of humanity: a large cranial structure to house a brain that is quite large for the size of the creature, small teeth, the development of a fully upright stance, hands with opposable thumbs, etcetera.

Our bones define us. They define the limits and character of our movement and our potential. The process of learning to reorganize our movements and use our skeletons in ways closer to the ideal improves our ability to be aware and, thus, improves the efficiency of our action and the quality, ease, and power of our lives.

. . .

CONFIDENCE AND THE SKELETON: EMBODYING POTENTIAL

Potential (the innate ability you have but have not yet used) and intention (a decision to use some of that potential) are the foundation of the New Fitness Pyramid. Intention is closely allied with belief. In other words, in order to effectively take action, you must believe the action is possible. As you saw in Section 2, there are two kinds of belief. One is the innate belief or confidence in your humanity and in your particular gifts. The second is the increase in confidence you get by experience as you work toward mastering a particular skill. Of the two, the first is more important because it focuses on stopping, feeling, and sensing what you already have. Without this kind of confidence, you will not start well. The process of developing the second kind of confidence follows and becomes mandatory for being fully confident. Eventually, the two types of confidence must be integrated. But the first kind is the starting point.

Nothing in the way of human fitness happens without confidence that it can be done. Fortunately, belief is not something you have to find or conjure up. It is part of our nature. It is a deep knowing. Just as you know that you can take the next breath, you know that you have unused capability. You may not be used to sensing this. You may have spent many years in situations that stifle creativity or that force you to act in an overly humble manner. Lay all that aside for a few minutes before you read the rest of this chapter. Be still and think of a time or a particular area in which you did or can feel innate ability. It is there. If you lay aside social conditioning, you will find a storehouse of knowing. When you can do something, you'll have a sense of power, a sense of ease. Cultivate that feeling.

Contemplate the following quote by French psychologist Émile Coué: "Every day in every way I am getting better and better."[95] Coué was famous for introducing this kind of auto suggestion. It was meant to be said at the beginning and ending of each day in a focused, relaxed, accepting manner. Can you see how profound this simple statement is and what its benefits are? Incorporating the meaning of this thinking into your life is tantamount to already having the benefits you desire. Sense and feel your innate ability without letting conflicting thoughts interfere. When you do this, you are ready to release some of your potential.

Can you see that the evidence of human potential is in your skeleton? Can you see how effort gets in the way of assuming a proper standing position? No matter how much muscular tension we put into trying to stand well, it is immersion in the process of sensing and feeling that helps us to release energy efficiently, not the effort to try harder that brings us closer bit by bit to the ideal of standing.

---

95 Coué, Émile. *My Method*, by Arthur A. Leidecker, BCH, Carpentersville, Illinois (1999), http://www.artleidecker.com/wp-content/uploads/2015/04/Coue_My_Method_12-20-99.pdf

Sensing and feeling require practice and experimentation. Once the vertical position is sensed, it is easier to use stored (potential) energy to release ourselves into movement. The same is true for standing in good emotional alignment. This requires balancing the demands of the environment. It's a kind of mental standing with the abstract mind open and ready to focus on new learning. An open mind is a source of potential energy. A closed mind is like a battery on a shelf that never gets used. We can practice being opened-minded and ready.

The same is true of belief or confidence. It is immersion in the process of sensing and feeling what is innately present that builds confidence. It is in learning to focus on what can truly be instead of the insecurities that take our attention away that builds us up. Building confidence can be practiced just as standing efficiently can be practiced. When learning to improve our standing position and sense of skeletal support in movement, can you see how your confidence can grow? You are *embodying* skilled use of your potential.

As always, fitness is practical, and what could be more concrete than your bones? If we think in terms of structure being related to function over time, then the skeleton is mineralized, calcified habits of action and thought. As it turns out, using our skeletons well is the key to good movement. When it comes to ideal movement, our skeleton provides support when gravity acts upon it, leaving our muscles free for movement and giving us a sense of lightness. Our skeleton supports our high center of gravity (the boulder) in a temporarily balanced position between movements. A feeling of heaviness is often the result of under-reliance on the skeleton for support (as if you were using muscle power to keep the boulder balanced on top of the hill).

• • •

INTENTION AND THE SKELETON IN ACTION

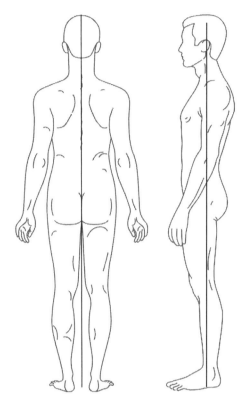

Using the skeleton to stand in vertical alignment is a basis for human functioning. It is the beginning point of all movement.

Figure 16.2. Image by: Anna Rassadnik

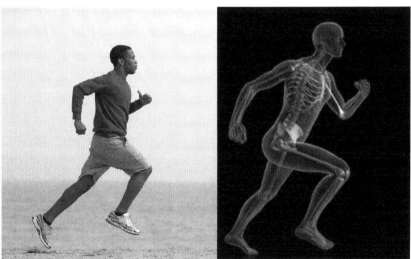

Figure 16.3. The skeleton in action—m-imagephotography commotion_design

But in order to align ourselves with an intention, it is necessary to think of action, not static standing. Movement must be involved, movement of some sort toward our intention. Let's take the idea of human functioning into practical movement. Humans are not built for standing. Our verticality and small base of support and relatively high center of gravity mean we can initiate movement quickly because of the kinetic energy stored in a center of gravity high above our feet. You can see this for yourself quite easily.

When you run or do all other movements that are possible, you do not remain vertical at all times, but the object is still to find the most effective path to transmit force through the joints. That means that whatever you are doing, the force used is transmitted through the center of the joints, not the edges only; the forces involved are transmitted through the joints and not at right angles to them.

Some people seem to stand and move elegantly, but most of us don't adopt the most successful postures all the time, even though efficiently using our skeleton is a way to maximize our potential. Why not? The answer lies in habit, conflicting intentions, and a lack of information about how to do otherwise. It is quite accurate to say that the way we move reflects our whole self: Emotional, physical, and mental habits are all displayed in movement. Keeping in mind mind-body unity, can you see that changing the way you stand and move can literally affect your potential in all areas?

You cannot do something and its opposite at the same time. You cannot stand vertically and easily and be insecure. You would physically express those two things differently; there would be something *off* in your posture and carriage. In terms of our physical action, we find resistance. This resistance can express itself as extra muscle contractions, the use of muscle that is extraneous to the action performed.

When we don't know how to do something well, we rely on old, ineffective habits. Inefficient action is a form of resistance, the same as using an inefficient conductor in an electrical circuit. The master uses less energy to execute a certain action than does the beginner.

. . .

HINDRANCES TO ALIGNING WITH INTENTION

The idea behind the word "align" is to place, or order, objects in a straight line. The idea of alignment is the intention to act in a certain way. The enactment of alignment involves awareness. Awareness is the ability to know the current condition of the system. Awareness then is the basis for aligning. In order to do what we want, especially if we want to do a new thing—something that uses more of our potential—all our actions and thoughts must be consistent, ordered in the same line of travel. And now we uncover the problem of conflicting thoughts, emotions, and actions. The difficulty is illustrated in Figure 16.4 by the two people in a canoe paddling in opposite directions. The work of one cancels out the work of the other, and no progress is made.

Figure 16.4. Hindrances to alignment—Kmimtz66

The example of the canoe is another example of *resistance*. Our habitual actions and movements unfold in uncoordinated action. We watch the runner who wants to move forward but wastes a lot of energy with side-to-side movements. Our thoughts and feelings want several things at once: I want to lose weight, but I want a piece of chocolate cake. I want to get some writing done, but I want to check Facebook. I want to run or climb well, but I don't want to spend time learning how, so my movements lack quality.

Action is, therefore, difficult. We don't experience the subjective feeling of ease and power because of internal friction and resistance.

How shall we solve this problem? We can only do so through heighted self-awareness. We have internal territory to explore. It's another example of the necessity of committing to a learning process. Trained weight lifters learned how to lift heavy weights. That means they know how to do it; they have experience and adaptation on their side. Experience and adaptation breed confidence. Confidence reduces internal conflict and doubt and contributes to neurological efficiency by recruiting muscle fibers. It takes awareness and experience in a situation to unleash your true strength.

Conflicting thoughts or motivations are not the source of a unified will. They are the mark of not being truly aligned with our intention. They produce inner conflict, not inner ease. This territory, this exploration, this pathway to ease by eliminating inner obstacles and conflicts is the great drama, the essence of the human journey. It is the elimination of obstacles that will make you great, not the application of more effort to overcome inefficient action.

We eliminate obstacles by being single-minded. We move more efficiently by learning to eliminate unnecessary effort. In both cases, we stop rowing in two directions at the same time.

Remember the biblical thought repeated by Abraham Lincoln: "A house divided against itself cannot stand."

Six-time Mr. Olympia winner, actor, and former governor of California, Arnold Schwarzenegger, used to give seminars to help other people succeed. He would ask a participant to state why they wanted to work out. If someone answered that they would like to work out so that if they became muscular, maybe they would enter a bodybuilding competition, he would tell them to sit down and that their answer was not correct. There is no *maybe*.

He would tell them that what is necessary is not to say, "I hope I can do it," but "I will do anything that it takes."[96] That is commitment. That is revaluing and putting away distractions. That is a unified will. That is coordinated mental action. And that requires learning to unmask what is inherently yours and pursuing only that.

The difference between Arnold and his competitors was that while the others wanted to get their training done each day, Arnold reveled in his. Rather than grimacing, he smiled as he worked knowing that each session, each moment, was getting him closer to his goal—the things he envisioned for himself. The difference between those who try harder and those who immerse themselves in the process with commitment and joy as they lay aside all distractions is dramatic. This is the foundational attitude to start with and, when necessary, returned to again and again.

A unified mind-body and the pursuit of awareness through movement are our greatest tool because all our conflicts are reflected in our movements, and all our movements affect our thoughts and feelings. Conflicts we experience in movement express themselves as excess muscular tension, tension that prevents us from acting fluidly. The skeleton is our support system, our flexible lightweight girders and beams. When we use our skeletons well, we feel "light on our feet." We move with ease.

---

96 Schwarzenegger, Arnold, "Arnold Schwarzenegger's Keys to Success," Million Dollar Baby Fitness (October 1, 2012), https://www.youtube.com/watch?v=UOUVkISESKc

This is the foundation, because any time we use our skeletons in inefficient ways, we waste energy and our movements suffer.

If you want to be better at sport or at anything else, improve the way you use your skeleton. Let it support and contribute to your movement and improve the way you move your center of gravity. If you use your skeleton better, you will find that your movements improve.

Likewise, if you want to use no more psychic energy than necessary, learn to commit. We can define commitment as the bones of our intentions. We can say that to commit is to act in ways that support our dreams, not in ways that distract us from them. Commitment is accepting a course of action, a change in appraisal, and reduces the value we place on things that distract us from what we want.

Potential is something you have. It can be used or remain unused as we choose. Allowing potential to flow is largely a matter of learning. It's a focus on removing obstacles and the ability to sense and feel improvement within ourselves. Using our potential opens us up to a world of possibilities. Instead of having only one way of doing things, we learn many ways to function in many situations. Potential is realized in action and not in static postures.

· · ·

POTENTIAL: ULTIMATE FITNESS, INFINITE POSSIBILITIES

The concepts of fitness, dynamic balance, and true flexibility are illustrated in this quote by Mabel Todd: "The intelligence of an individual may be measured by the speed with which he orients himself to new situations."[97]

To react quickly, we can't be biased toward any one habit or direction. Remember that for primitive man, the ability to move without hesitation in any direction was a survival skill. Within our inner life, the aim is to avoid being too rigid, to be able to move without restricting ourselves so we can adapt to and overcome difficulties in our environment. It can even be said that we have the ability to transcend difficulties if we are fluid enough in our inner movement, if we do not resist ourselves, and if we inhibit our unnecessary habits. We start from a position of neutrality—not biased in any particular direction—and then we can respond quickly and appropriately to the situations we face.

Jeff Haller says that "true biological fitness is reflected in one's capacity to move with agility and without hesitation from any starting position to any other orientation. This type of fitness comes about through methodical and painstaking exploration in as many positions as can be imagined, and with clear functional goals in mind."[98] This is true flexibility. Now we have introduced the ultimate complexity: movement in any direction at any time. Thus, we can consider being ready to move up, down, left, right, forward, and/or backward at any time. This is more than enough territory to explore for a lifetime.

To explore our potential to this extent is extraordinary and is the greatest example of life fitness, maintaining a kind of neutral dynamic balance, ready to unleash our potential. Think of the greatest

97 Todd, Mabel Ellsworth; *The Thinking Body: Study of the Balancing Forces of Dynamic Man*; Gestalt Journal Press, Gouldsboro, ME (2008)

98 Yu, Edward; *The Mass Psychology of Fittism: Fitness, Evolution and the First Two Laws of Thermodynamics*; Undocumented Worker Press (2015) 329

running backs who epitomize the ability to change direction faster than any defender can counter; the great writer who has freed himself from a love of his words and is able to discard a chapter, even a whole book and rewrite, re-create according to a new vision, one closer to his true intent; the martial artist who can pop up seemingly effortlessly from the ground from any position; the runner who can shift gears seamlessly and understands the moment in which to do it; the person who is free from any one emotional state, who can shift emotional gears to handle the moment; the beauty of the greatest dancer; the rock climber who solves the challenges of a rock face like they are pieces of a puzzle, not holding rigidly to one way of doing things but exploring every possible handhold and change of position; the person who has prepared intensely over a long period of time and then focuses to stand up and speak to a group while mobilizing all their resources to be present for the audience.

Now think of some area in your life in which you would like to explore more, to enjoy more, to develop your gifts in. Each and every one of these examples is an example of personal refinement. The ability to move from one position to another without hesitation both metaphorically and physically is the ability to refine yourself, to refine your craft, your personal expression, your life. There is no perfect, only better. Therefore, your potential is limitless.

The experience of learning expands our possibilities not because of what we learn but because we learn, because we *can* learn. The moment we are faced with something new is a humbling moment, a moment of not knowing, of wanting to go back to what we already know, to cling to the old. Being ready to move in any direction at any time means we have confidence that we *can* learn. The desire to go backward to the familiar gives way to enjoyment of being open to the new. We know that we have the freedom to go this way or that.

It may seem overwhelming to be turned loose to explore the infinite, but don't worry. Each discipline, each activity, each skill you want to explore, no matter what it is—athletics, mathematics, art, music, relationships—has fundamentals. There is a beginning place. Discover the fundamentals, and you will have direction in your exploration.

For example, the fundamentals of running include keeping a long, non-compressed spine; lifting your knees by using your psoas muscles or main hip flexor; pelvic rotation; trunk counterrotation; and hip extension. Once you master the fundamentals, you still have a world of exploration to create harmonious, integrated, self-expressive movements. Exploration is a step-by-step process, so start with the first step, the fundamentals. The fundamentals are the *what* of your learning. The detail, the experiences, and personal discoveries are the *how* of your learning. There are always finer and finer distinctions to make, finer and finer hows to explore. There is no limit to the amount of improvement you can make.

But what does mastering the feat of being able to move in any direction at a moment's notice get us? Why does it matter? It matters because we use movement as a tool to improve our lives, to find more enjoyment, to be poised to act appropriately to each situation so we can do the things we want to do. Be ready to respond to each situation appropriately, and you will survive, thrive, and prosper. Respond in a less organized manner, and you will not recognize all the possibilities available to you. Our ability to move physically and mentally is a powerful tool that helps us to create possibilities in life.

Unleashing potential—efficiently following our intention—is the foundation of the New Fitness Pyramid. We can learn all these skills; they are not natural talents handed to a precious few. The New Fitness Pyramid offers a process for learning how to do this.

CHAPTER 16 LESSON:

ORGANIZE YOUR SKELETON TO CARRY A HEAVY WEIGHT ON YOUR HEAD

According to the New Fitness Pyramid, human potential is dependent upon efficient movement, specifically good use of the skeleton. Remember how important it was for our ancestors to maintain good posture so they could see above the grass and move quickly in response to opportunities and threats? Modern humans rely on the same skeletal system and must, therefore, keep it well organized and strong (use the inherent strength of the bones). Can you imagine needing to support or carry a heavy weight on your head like some people still do to transport water and other loads without damaging or straining your neck? In this lesson, you'll learn how practical this is because it changes your thinking and sense of how to use your skeleton. You may not ever carry a heavy weight on your head, but when thinking about this (and lifting other heavy objects), many people think about pressing into the ground rather than rising up.

• • •

Take your time: Allow 15–20 minutes to complete this lesson.

1. Stand and slowly organize yourself from head to toe as if you need to support this kind of weight. Does the crown of your head rise to support and align with the weight rather than collapse under it?

2. Walk around while entertaining this idea of supporting weight on your head and sense your weight on your feet. What has changed in how you organize your body? How does your weight feel on your feet now? Do you have a clearer idea of how your skeleton can support you?

3. Return to standing. Now, let's examine in more detail the idea of carrying a weight on your head. Your skeleton is charged with the job of holding you up all day. If you imagine carrying a heavy weight on your head, you will learn something about holding yourself upright, balanced and easy, in the field of gravity without carrying weight on your head.

   Start with the crown of your head. It is obvious that some positions are inappropriate for supporting weight. If you bring your chin down toward your chest, you can feel that a 40-pound weight would greatly increase the strain on your neck and that your neck would not balance the weight efficiently—not to mention the effect it would have on your breathing.

4. Instead of bringing your chin toward your chest, allow the crown of your head to rise gently toward the sky. It turns out that the best way to support weight on your head is to rise into it. You have seven vertebrae in your neck. Image each very gently rising up into the weight. Now imagine that someone puts his hands on your shoulders and pushes straight down. Or, if a friend is handy, have them stand behind you and push down on your shoulders. This should be done gently so you can sense small changes. Do you feel a little collapse in your spine, perhaps a little give in some part, say your low back?

5. You have twelve vertebrae in your upper and five in your lower back. Try to use your imagination to organize each vertebra as if it must support a heavy weight that's been placed on your head. Start just below your neck and imagine them one by one until you reach your pelvis. Imagine each one, then all of them rising to support a weight. Continue to imagine your pelvis, legs, ankles, and feet aligning to support weight. Imagine again that someone is pushing gently down on your shoulders. Is there a change? With your new posture, can you support weight more easily?

6. How are you standing now? Now that you have better support through your skeleton, can you consciously let go of some of the muscles you think are holding you up? How much tension is necessary? How much tension do you have in the back of your neck?

The muscles of the spine and low back work to hold you erect. Can you stand with less tension in your low back? Your abdominal muscles are also postural stabilizers. Can you find a place where your belly is freer? What about the tension in your glutes, quadriceps, and lower legs? Perhaps you are now aware of a slightly lower tone in these muscles that constantly work to hold us up. Walk around again only to notice your body. Are you getting a clearer picture of how your skeleton works to support your body and its various functions? How will you use this image of your skeleton when moving other parts of your body? Can you feel that you are lighter on your feet when you use your skeleton well, when every bone is aligned to support you in gravity? How does your self-image change when you feel that you can stand without effort?

· · ·

Try going through a whole day maintaining an easy but long non-compressed spine, a more vertically oriented skeleton, one that counters the downward pull of gravity well, and see how much energy you save. Be easy; don't strain or try too hard to do this. You might be surprised at how much less energy you use. You might also find that it is difficult to counter the old habit of standing and moving with a skeleton that is slightly collapsed in the field of gravity, not efficiently aligned.

It can be difficult to find full skeletal support. It is more elusive than it might seem at first. You may need a Feldenkrais practitioner to help guide you, but experiment with this lesson and its more aligned way of standing and moving. Keep this visual in your mind: an aligned, relaxed image of a string attached to the crown of your head and everything hanging from that. You are not seeking perfection, not trying hard. You're just going to maintain an image of casual vertical standing or sitting. Do the work of retaining this image of alignment, and notice the difference at the end of the day.

CHAPTER 17

The New Fitness Pyramid: Process of Improvement

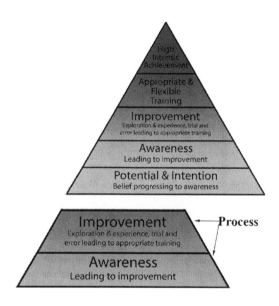

Figure 17.1. Awareness in process

You might notice that awareness has been included both in the foundation of the New Fitness Pyramid and also in the process. This is not a mistake as awareness is the transitional element between the potential in the foundation and the improvement in the process.

To understand the New Fitness Pyramid's process of improvement, let's return to the metaphor of space exploration by going back to the Apollo program. Apollo 13 was called NASA's most successful

failure. Perhaps you have watched the movie *Apollo 13*, the story of
the Apollo mission that failed to reach the moon due to an explosion in an oxygen tank during a routine procedure. After the explosion, the ground controllers were faced with a number of questions
about how to proceed. The first thing they needed to do was figure
out if the issue was caused by an instrumentation problem or if
there was physical damage to the spacecraft. Everyone was working
frantically when the mission commander, James Lovell, confirmed
that a gas of some sort—probably oxygen—was venting into space.
It became clear that the spacecraft was indeed badly damaged, and
what should have been a routine flight followed by a lunar landing
had turned into a battle for survival. It was clear that they had lost
critical oxygen, crucial electrical power, and that time was not on
their side.

I remember this drama being reported in the news. The whole
world watched to see what would happen. Yet, the danger the astronauts faced was greater than the general public was aware of. Imagine
being confined to the small space in the lunar excursion module
for several days, a space that was designed to be cramped quarters
for two men but now held three. The temperature had dropped to
about 38 degrees Fahrenheit, and the atmosphere inside the spacecraft was very damp: decidedly uncomfortable conditions. Add to
the discomfort the enormous complexity of getting the spacecraft
back to Earth. And if even one key decision had been faulty, the
astronauts would have used up their electrical power too soon and
suffocated, not have attained the trajectory needed to get back to
Earth, or not had the use of critical systems including parachutes
to reenter the Earth's atmosphere safely. It would be like three men
dying slowly in a refrigerator in view of everyone on Earth. Getting

the crew back to Earth as quickly and safely as possible was on the hearts and minds of everyone involved.

I will draw on two examples from the Apollo 13 incident. First, there was a lengthy debate about whether to turn the spacecraft around and bring it straight back to Earth (direct abort) or to use the Moon's gravity to slingshot the astronauts back to Earth (free-return trajectory). The debate went on for some time: Should they turn around or go forward?

As it turned out, the second option was safer because it did not rely on firing an engine that might have been damaged in the explosion, but it required more time. The astronauts ran the risk of running out of consumables before they returned home, but this option avoided an obvious danger and gave the controllers time to think and work on the problem.

The second relevant example is the debate about electrical power consumption and conservation. Young engineer John Aaron realized that conserving power was critical and that difficult decisions must be made about which systems to shut down and keep running. But, each contractor for the various spacecraft systems insisted that their system was essential and, therefore, needed to be prioritized. Aaron had to withstand all the arguments for keeping systems turned on but knew the numbers and stood his ground. Everything, meaning everything in the command module was to be shut down. Both the decision to continue around the moon and the radical decision to shut down the command module were instrumental in saving the astronauts' lives.

These two scenarios can be used to summarize the essential elements of the process segment of the New Fitness Pyramid. This section of the pyramid is about overcoming plateaus and releasing individual potential. This is something that can't be done with more effort alone. There are two points to be made. First, you must be willing to listen carefully to feedback from your mind and body in the environment and be willing to literally change direction if need be. Like the Apollo 13 astronauts, you are not going to the Moon this time. You may also need to change directions in a figurative sense in your practice or life. You must be willing to try something different when the old way of doing things is not working.

Second, you must have the courage to stand by and persist in the new direction as John Aaron did when he stood by the reality (the numbers) and against all the voices shouting not to shut this or that thing down. These two scenarios are part of the same story; they are integral parts of the story of the rescue of the men aboard the Apollo 13 spacecraft. And for you, they are a summary of the process your training must take. Listen carefully to the data coming in, or in your case, to the feedback you get from your mind and body in the environment. Rely on and trust your inner voice that senses and feels what you need to improve.

Let's return to Dick Fosbury and the "Fosbury Flop" as an example of being willing to pay close attention to bodily feedback and make changes. His willingness to do so brought him to an entirely new level way beyond what he might have originally expected when he was working with other styles. His body was telling him that he needed to raise his hips. It was always his hips that contacted and dislodged the bar. And as he followed that clue—that feedback—over time, he completely changed his style.

Sometimes, Dick Fosbury was laughed at, and his method of jumping seemed odd or humorous at first, but it didn't matter. He knew he was jumping better, and other people began to follow his lead and copy his style. It can be hard to do something new. Society has many functions and one is to encourage conformity. People tend to laugh at those who are different. But it is important to find your own style, your own voice.

There was another athlete who "did things all wrong." His reach was considered too short, he didn't set his feet to jab, and he didn't stand flatfooted and rely only on power like other heavyweights. But I remember him as a great athlete. The self-proclaimed "greatest of all time," three-time heavyweight champion of the world, Muhammad Ali. His training was legendary and innovative. His footwork was so beautiful and fluid. With great agility, he did indeed "float like a butterfly" around the ring. His artistry was so brilliant that he redefined heavyweight boxing, and his movements and style have yet to be equaled. He could move in any direction at any time.

He had his own voice. And what a voice it was: humorous, taunting, exuding commitment and confidence. He was serious about being the best. He had the courage of his convictions and went to jail as a conscientious objector during the Vietnam War, making him a social activist. He was a man who changed his name and his religion. Later, he became the public face of Parkinson's Disease. And the face of courage when his shaking hands lit the Olympic torch. He did not hide behind the mask society had given him or stay silent. Like him or not, he stood as a great athlete and an individual of influence. Never satisfied with mediocrity, he was a person who could shine in many of life's environments.

So there you have it. The two requirements for breaking through plateaus: (1) Pay careful attention to the feedback you get from your practice. Where is something not working? What specifically is not working? Be willing to change what you are doing, and (2) be willing to stand by the change; uphold it and persist in it. Have the courage to have your own voice.

Experiencing plateaus can be frustrating. It may lead you to think that, indeed, you have reached the limit of your abilities. You may have the desire to improve and are working hard to get closer to your ideal but find yourself at a dead end. Now, how do you move on? The answer is in what my dad used to say: "If something is not working, stop and figure it out. Don't force it." A deeper understanding of how to practice involves changing direction and finding a new way to approach what you are doing. Understanding how to change your practice comes through continual feedback, which reveals what works and what doesn't, thereby giving you direction about how to change your practice technique.

Figure 17.2. Scott Forrester

To make a point clear, the process of listening to and carefully following feedback is indeed the key to the aware athlete's progress, but you should know that this process is not a onetime thing. As Steve Backley, former world record javelin thrower says, "Successful sports people keep reinventing themselves. Whether you win or lose, you always need to get up to a new level—and you can't do that if you're always doing the same old thing."[99] We can call this continual refinement successive approximation. You experienced successive approximation in the lesson at the end of Chapter 10. You may remember going through several iterations of matching a word to a bodily sensation.

You cannot attain perfection, but every cycle of learning you do in your sport or life practice takes you just a little bit closer to your ideal, a little farther in the direction you want to go. Successive approximation means that there is a huge difference between the practice of a beginner and that of an elite performer. Think of the beginner just learning the rules of the game, the use of the equipment involved and a few simple strategies, and then look at the contrast between the beginner and the practice of a high-level performer who is refining his timing to the nth degree, making small differences that the beginner cannot even perceive. A beginner may be concerned with big movements and fast progress while the elite athlete cultivates the ability to slow down and learn. This continual search for smaller and smaller differences is what I call *the athlete's edge*.

• • •

99 BBC, "Lessons I've Learned from Steve Backley," BBC Sports (May 8, 2007), http://news.#1bbc.co.uk/sport2/hi/athletics/skills/6615335.stm

The Apollo 13 engineers in mission control had lots of data to look at. But they were in no rush for the quickest solution. They gave themselves time to become more and more intimate with the problems they were facing and to work out solutions that would save the lives of the crew members. Likewise, you will have lots of data: miles run, interval times, hills climbed, and especially the examples of others. But you are unique. Real progress for you will come when you become more and more intimate with yourself—when you recognize your own structure, your own voice, your own unique mind-body feedback and where it leads you. When you take a chance on following that inner guidance, you will be on a unique road that leads to inner strength. Moshe Feldenkrais encouraged students by saying, "Trust yourself to work out what is right for you."[100] He emphasized the importance of learning, the result of which is improved action. We also learn by taking new actions. New ways of acting help us learn, and acting in new ways results in learning. The two are connected.

· · ·

The poem below highlights the benefits of improvement through self-awareness. It is about using the strength of your bones to produce a sense of lightness; less muscular effort; more efficient movement that works better for you; and being aligned with your own structure, your own intention instead of trying harder and listening only to external voices that hinder your ability to listen to yourself. It's about learning the difference between unnecessary effort that does not work well for you and effort that is efficient and easy. It is

100 Feldenkrais, Moshe, "Self Discovery for You" (2010-2017), http://www.self-discovery-for-you.com/moshe-feldenkrais.html

the difference between trying and learning to improve. By making these distinctions, we can organize ourselves more effectively in all areas, and we can strengthen our inner voice so we can hear our own authentic mind-body feedback.

. . .

Inner Strength

Strengthen your core and stand up straight!
Is that all there is to the perfect gait?
Work harder to achieve the correct form.
Get everything adjusted to the norm,
Then test and you will see
There is more to freedom than meets the eye.
Perfection is an illusion for us,
Yet with our acting we continually fuss.
With ourselves we continually fight.
We try and we try yet we only get tight.
We've done everything right
But here we stand
And now we need a deeper guide
One that comes from the inside
Not imposed from without
Because here we stand
With an empty feeling of something missing
There is something more that we can't find
We know that kicked football should sail so far
Yet somehow, we miss the magic sweet spot
Somehow, we know we can lift more than that
We grit the teeth and try harder than before

Yet our leverages are not working the best

We know we can run faster than this

We push and push

Yet the feeling persists

Deep down we know there is more there than this

Here we are on this flat plateau

But way inside there is more, there is more.

We cannot go on this way any farther

And then we see there is another way.

We have the ideal

But now we know

It cannot be attained

It is only a guiding star

A clear direction

And with a clearer appreciation of the infinite

We also know, there is no end to improvement

There is never just perfect

But there is always better

There is even excellent

It is not by force

But by learning

It is alignment

Alignment of the skeleton in gravity

Alignment of bones with the direction of force

Alignment with your most personal self

We cease to try harder and now we are, now we are listening

To the waves of information awareness is bringing

To the details, the new combinations, the experiments

That lead to new patterns

And access to what we find, deep inside, deep inside
To personal discovery, and then we can
Make it easy we can make it light
We feel our bones and commit our mind
We open ourselves to the process, putting ego aside.
With eyes now open wide
We add to our movement repertoire, and gain the ability
To make new choices, to move in any direction
We adapt, we morph, we change
We focus the mind to do this or that
With inner voice, inner confidence, inner strength
And then unlimited power we find.
We act according to our self-image, they say
To truly improve, you must get out of your own way.
Laying aside distractions, and obstacles
Beliefs that hinder.
Then we will see what was always there
Something to get us from here to there
Personal gift and power
Our dreams have been hiding in plain sight
Pull back the veil and you will take flight!

. . .

We face unpleasant circumstances sometimes, so who wouldn't want to live an easier, more powerful life? This is not to say that your life will be easy. The point is that a well-organized, better coordinated movement or action is easier than an action that is poorly organized, and improvement is never ending. With good organization, you can do things that would otherwise be impossible. You will be able to run farther than you once thought you could. You will stay focused in the heat of a championship match. You will be able to get up off the floor when you are old. You can improve anything you encounter in life. When well-organized movement becomes foundational to your action, you will save energy and be able to use it for activities that allow you to live life fully and will have reserves to use when supreme effort is called for. You will become your most effective self. You will uncover your inner voice, the only source of personal confidence.

Successive approximation is the practice of doing the hard things and making them easier. Then you can do the really hard things. Remember when you first did something that seemed hard, like riding a bicycle? After a short time, it wasn't hard anymore, then you were able to develop more skill in riding. You can't get far without putting in the focused, feedback-driven practice to make the fundamentals easy. Eventually you will be able to make the really hard things look easy to an observer. And who wouldn't want to be able to be more effective in life, to line themselves up, to align with their goals, their dreams? Isn't that what everyone wants?

Everyone struggles to overcome obstacles and to develop real-world resilience and confidence. It is your own very real story, your large and small victories, that brings value to your life and overflows to build confidence in others. And as you learn how to use personal awareness to improve, to find and do the things that work for you, and when you have inner direction, you are ready to put together appropriate training, training that is right for you.

CHAPTER 17 LESSON:
IMPROVE YOUR DEAD LIFT

After much discussion of the process of improvement, this lesson is a practical example of improving the basic human act of lifting. We all need to lift things occasionally, so learning how to do so is time well spent. I will use the dead lift in a gym context for illustrative purposes. You'll learn to do the hip-hinge movement, use your powerful glutes, and take care of your back.

• • •

Take your time: Allow 45 minutes to complete this lesson. You'll need a chair, broomstick, and well-padded surface that's comfortable enough to work on for several minutes. Work through each part carefully and with awareness to develop good form. Rest whenever you need to and when prompted to do so in the lesson.

Figure 17.3

Figure 17.4

Figure 17.5

Figure 17.6

Part 1: Lift in a Quadruped Position

1. Begin this lesson on all fours in quadruped position. Do not let your low back and abdomen sag excessively. Do you feel stable in this position? Keep your hands directly under your shoulders and your hips aligned vertically over your knees. Shift a little of your weight toward your left shoulder, then your right shoulder, then toward one leg, then the other. Can you lift only your right arm up from the mat?

2. Lift your hand straight up a little ways. You may bend your elbow. How did you do it? Did you mainly bend your elbow, or did you raise your hand somehow by lifting your shoulder blade? Try it both ways. Put your right hand down, and repeat the movement of lifting your hand many times. How is your sense of support on your other three limbs?

3. Rest on your back.

4. Come to all fours and lift your left hand many times. How is this side different? How did you organize yourself to do this? Did you bend your elbow? Did you lift your hand by lifting your shoulder blade? Did you lean to the right side? Try several ways of lifting your hand. What was your support through your other three limbs like?

5. Rest.

6. Lift your right leg above the mat, and put it down many times. Can you feel a different self-organization when you do this? Lift your left leg many more times. Can you feel how you shift your weight to do these movements? Can you feel the way the mus-

cles of your abdominal region, back, glutes, and legs organize themselves to do these movements?

7. Lift an arm or leg one or two more times to see if the movements and your body's organization is clearer.

8. Rest on your back.

Part 2: Walk with Your Hands Close to Your Knees

1. Return to all fours, and walk your hands very close to your knees. Now lift both hands and then come to a tall kneeling position. Did you feel the stabilizing muscles of your torso help you do this? Did you feel the relationship of the sternum and pelvis when you moved?

2. Lower yourself down to all fours with your hands directly in front of your knees. Walk your hands forward until your hands are again under your shoulders. Now, walk your hands back toward your knees, but leave slightly more room between your hands and knees (maybe just a couple of inches more) this time.

3. Again, lift yourself to a tall kneeling position. There is something very important to be aware of here: Notice how the work your abdominals must do to stabilize your torso as you raise yourself increases. This stabilizing work is an important part of the dead-lift move.

4. Experiment with lifting yourself when your hands are farther and farther from your knees. Take a great deal of care to do only quality movements. Do only what is easy and clear to you, and notice how the work of the muscles that stabilize your trunk increases each time you move your hands farther away from your knees.

5. Lie down and rest on your back.

Part 3: Easily Rise from a Chair and Hover in Comfort

1. Sit in a chair and slowly stand. Can you do this slow movement with ease? Begin to descend to sit in the chair, but when you are halfway to sitting, stop and rest your hands on your thighs.

2. Look easily to the left and then to the right several times. Is your normal low-back curve preserved, with no excessive sag or rounding occurring, as you rest your hands on your thighs for support?

3. Come to standing again in front of the chair. Place your feet hip width apart. Begin to bend your knees and hips as if to sit in the chair. Stop halfway down.

4. Place the midpoint of your forearms on your thighs and look right and left. See if you can find comfort in this position. Can you organize your whole self to be comfortable here for a few moments? Picture yourself in a stance like a linebacker before the beginning of a play.

5. Experiment with ways you can come to standing from this position. Can you keep a neutral spine—using the support of the muscles that stabilize your torso in the same way you did when you came to a tall kneeling position a few moments ago—as you rise? It is important to sense the relationship between the sternum and the pelvis as you come to standing. As you sit back toward the chair, your lower legs stay vertical. The important movement to notice is around your hip joints. Can you keep your lower legs vertical, or is this difficult for you? In order to do this, your buttocks need to move backward toward the chair at the same time your torso bends forward at the hips to balance the weight of your pelvis as it moves backward.

When you decide to rise from a chair, your torso first leans forward, bending at the hip joints while your lower legs stay vertical.

After your pelvis begins to rise from the chair, it comes forward and your sternum moves up and backward. The movement is around your hip joints, not your back. Make sure that you are creating the same hip-hinge movement that you experienced when you were on all fours at the beginning of this lesson. Carry this learning into the next part.

6.   Rest.

Part 4: Use the Hip-Hinge Movement to Lower Your Hands

1.   Come to standing with your feet about hip width apart. Begin to bend your hips and knees while keeping your lower legs close to vertical. Your hips will go backward as if to sit in a chair. Can you maintain balance as you lower yourself into the beginning of a squat? Do this several times. Pay attention to the movement and the relative position of your sternum in relation to your pelvis. Does your balance improve as you practice awareness of these things?

The next time you begin to lower yourself into a squat, run your hands down the outsides of your legs. Can you go a little lower on your legs each time you do the movement until your hands are about 18 inches above the floor? When you perform a dead lift, your hands will be on a bar that is not in contact with the floor.

2.   Lie down and rest on your back.

Part 5: Rise from a Chair with Your Palms on the Floor

1.   Sit in a chair again.

2.   Reach toward the floor with your palms down and arms on the outsides of your legs and ankles. Go only as far as is comfortable.

3.   Now, place both of your palms on the floor in front of you. To make this easy, you may feel that your pelvis needs to rise from

the seat a little. Lower your pelvis and sit gently. Repeat the movement of raising your pelvis and touching the floor in front of you several times. Do the movement smoothly.

4. On your last move, stand up instead of sitting in the chair. Sit in the chair. Now lift your pelvis slightly and place your palms to the floor. Stand up instead of sitting back down. This is very similar to the dead-lift movement. Repeat this movement several times.

Part 6: Lift a Bar

You will need a broom handle, dowel, or piece of PVC pipe to simulate a barbell for this part of the lesson. It is possible to imagine holding onto a barbell, but try to find something to hold onto. (For the purpose of this explanation, I will assume you're using a broom handle.)

1. Stand and hold onto your choice of bar with both hands. Place your feet about hip width apart, and hold onto the broomstick with a grip that is just wider than the placement of your legs.

2. Descend into a squat. Are you comfortable as you lower the stick to about 18 inches above the floor? Do you maintain your normal low-back curvature with no rounding or excessive arching of your back? Can you keep your head in line with your spine? Are your hips low but comfortable?

3. Imagine that you are holding a heavy weight. Hang your arms straight down. Do not lift a heavy weight with your arms. Do not bend your elbows as you lift. Your knuckles should face forward; your palms should face backward.

4. Come to a standing position, and imagine that you have a heavy weight in your hands. Note the relationship between your pelvis and sternum as you did in the previous lesson. The power of the

lift is in your hips. Your head must rise as you look forward and complete the lift at the same time your pelvis comes forward. The motion is in the hips. Your knees should not move toward each other during the lift. Do not initiate the movement with a rounded back; keep your back long. This hip-hinge movement has been emphasized in many ways in this lesson.

5. Use your glutes to bring your hips up and forward to start the lift and finish it in a full standing position. Keep your back long and all the motion in your hip joint. Your stance should remain balanced throughout the lift. Do this lift many times while imagining how you would organize yourself to lift a heavy weight.

6. Rest.

7. Stand and take hold of the broomstick again. As you descend into the lifting position, sense whether you are positioning yourself to use the maximum power of your hips to lift a heavy weight. Are your hips too low to begin to get the weight off the ground? The initial movement of this lift may require you to raise your hips slightly to a more advantageous position. This is all one movement, but you may feel the initiation of the movement in your hips.

8. Finish the movement by bringing your pelvis forward and your sternum up and back. Your head will rise, and you will use the stabilizing muscles of your trunk and back like you did when you rose from all fours to tall kneeling when you performed the movements in Part 1 of this exercise. In this movement, however, you will feel more power generated.

· · ·

Even if you have been performing dead lifts for a while, take time to experiment with a weight that feels quite light to you. Sense how to initiate the lift. Try many variations. Squat with low hips and begin the lift. Next, try to slightly unbend your hips and knees by slightly raising your hips to initiate the movement. Find what is most powerful for you. Proceed very, very gradually toward heavier weights. You may want to start with a standard bar that weighs about 20 pounds or an Olympic bar, which weighs 40 pounds. Learning to lift properly and powerfully will serve you well as you explore and interact with your environment.

CHAPTER 18

The New Fitness Pyramid: Fitness and Training as a Learning Experience

You have awareness. You have learned to enter the cycle of exploration-feedback-performance again and again and again. It is the basis of your training. You esteem the patient acquisition of skills more than the superficial application of brute force. You understand that nothing is accomplished passively; nothing is accomplished complacently. A strong desire to learn is necessary for any athlete-human to succeed.

Complacency, the opposite of a burning desire to learn, is a kind of self-satisfaction that ignores the actual situation and says, I am satisfied with the way things are. Complacency negates your training efforts. When we are complacent, we do not make progress.

Awareness, on the other hand, is real-world knowing of exactly what is available to you in the moment. Awareness is knowledge of what the endless possibilities are if you apply your gifts. With real moment-by-moment perception of what is, you know what to do and how to do it. You can do what it takes to be faithful to who you really are, to what you really are meant to be. So, start your training. What it takes to fully express yourself is within you. You can express your inherent self through the things you are most interested in, the things you care most about.

Now you are ready to do the work. Now you know how to train. Now you are ready to overcome the obstacles in your way. And there will be obstacles that are as real for you as the lion on the savanna was to your ancestors. When you learn new things, there will be confusion until the new becomes familiar. When you use more of your potential, when you set high goals, you will wonder if you have what it takes to finish what you started. You will move outside your comfort zone, and it will be humbling. You will experience highs and lows. You will be like the ultra-runner who comes to the end of his resources both physical and mental and thinks that he can't go on before a friend, another runner, comes along, takes his hand, and says, "You've got this," and they go on to finish the race.

At the heart of your training is your ability to overcome obstacles. Encourage yourself along the way by reminding yourself of what you have already been through. Embrace the process, get real experience, and surprise yourself.

Figure 18.1. Appropriate and flexible training

Appropriate training is indeed a real-world learning experience and deserves specific examples. Suppose you want to be a runner, rock climber, football player, musician, artist, writer, or scientist. A person who practices their craft under varied conditions and experiments with many ways of doing things; synthesizes all the information that comes their way; takes the actions apart; reintegrates the pieces; and forms new, more satisfying patterns will be a good runner, rock climber, football player, musician, writer, or scientist. A person who focuses on exercise—movement for movement's sake; thought for thought's sake; or, more generally, doing for doing's sake even when it seems useful while neglecting the skills they need to develop in their chosen path—will be a poor runner, rock climber, musician, artist, writer, scientist, husband, wife, son, daughter, or friend. A person who practices their craft with awareness and commitment and who adds complementary activities may have the best of both worlds. A football player may add weight training and become even better if they do not neglect their blocking, throwing, and mental game skills. Writers and artists, scientists and performers will be even better when they absorb the work of others in their fields provided they don't neglect their own skills. It is useless to add exercise as a substitute for skill. Even in rehab, the hierarchy remains: Strength training, for instance, is no substitute for learning a better stride.

• • •

PREREQUISITES FOR TRAINING: POTENTIAL, BELIEF, AWARENESS, AND IMPROVEMENT

By now you should recognize your inherent human potential.

But nothing happens without belief that it can. This is where you envision yourself succeeding. This is the practice of confidence as you focus on the vision of what you want in daily, persistent, practical ways. "Living your best life begins with knowing what you really want out of life."[101] And as Socrates has been quoted as having said, "The secret to change is to focus all of your energy, not on fighting the old but on building the new."[102] This principle is timeless and serves high achievers today. Oprah Winfrey encourages us to "create the highest grandest vision possible for your life, because you become what you believe."[103]

Belief is the foundation of it all. If these saying don't challenge you and make you just a little uncomfortable, I don't know what will. I don't mind admitting that I am just beginning to see what is possible and the adventure that awaits me. And, like all adventurers, I experience nervous excitement. We will stand and face the lion.

Here is a quick formula for adventure:

Step 1—See something that seems awesome and say That would be fun or meaningful.

Step 2—Arrive at the figurative or literal starting line feeling some trepidation because we are challenging ourselves after all. We think, Am I crazy?

Step 3—Finish the challenge and think, Wow, I did it.

Step 4—Repeat steps 1 through 3.

· · ·

101 Canfield, Jack and Dr. Peter Chee, *Coaching for Breakthrough Success: Proven Techniques for Making Impossible Dreams Possible,* McGraw Hill Education, New York (2013) 123

102 Millman, Dan, *Way of the Peaceful Warrior: A Book that Changes Lives*, H. J. Kramer (1984)

103 https://www.goodreads.com/quotes/625783-create-the-highest-grandest-vision-possible-for-your-life-because

Awareness, a special form of abstract thinking, defines the highest level of human functioning. This is one of the most important ideas in this book.

We live a physical life in a physical body. The brain itself is part of our body. The spiritual aspect of life, that which transcends, is played out in our physical bodies. We act not simply through logic but through emotion, habit, and unconscious experience. The result of which is action. Action is movement, and movement expresses our entire organization even at an unconscious level. Movement is the window to the self, and awareness is our ability to observe ourselves through our movements in the environment and is the essential tool for self-improvement.

The experience of mind-body unity—of learning to observe and to sense and feel ourselves—is where we become process oriented, where we lay the foundations of our success, where we make the fine distinctions that make all the difference in how we navigate life and interact with our environment. This connection is what gives us the power to do whatever we want. Increasing our self-awareness is necessary to move more easily; to learn the fine details and the how of what we do; to stay more vital as we age; to improve our performance in sport and life; and to sense and feel our core, the center of ourselves, the power of the pelvis. The ability to improve the way we move in order to overcome pain and physical limitation is overlooked by most people. We step on the same spot year after year and wonder why we hurt and are over-whelmed when we finally see the liberating difference learning to move more appropriately makes.

. . .

Life is a process. Learning is a process based on trial and error; listening; observing the parts and the whole; slowing down and making finer distinctions; and innovating, making your own discoveries. No one can teach you anything. Learning is an organic process based on your own experience. Direction comes from within. Relying too heavily on external guidance can only hinder your learning.

"Trust the experts" is false advice if trusting the experts means abdicating responsibility for the learning process. Assuming the responsibility for your own learning greatly increases the chances of surviving and thriving in any environment. Remember that everything originates inside, or within, you. Your response to circumstances, your view of life is all an internal journey. When and if you learn to hear and express your own voice, you can open up the world of shared knowledge as in the next step. Improvement begins and ends with self-awareness. Begin here and the next steps follow.

. . .

APPROPRIATE TRAINING: A CONCRETE PROCESS

Set goals but don't hold to them rigidly. Stay self-aware. Remember that training yourself to do something well is an incremental process.

If you need information, get it. So much is available now, a lot of it for free. Read books. Watch instructional videos. Observe the skill others demonstrate.

Open yourself up to one of the most powerful human experiences, the sharing of knowledge. Get a teacher. Take a course. Hire a coach. Partner with a mentor. See a somatic practitioner. Find one who fits your current needs and whose approach resonates with you. If the road to what you want has a required path, take it. We open up the whole repository of human knowledge and experience when we stop going it alone.

If you need a training plan, get one. There are plenty of resources to do just that. Be disciplined enough to follow it and flexible enough to listen to your own needs. Contrary to what might be advertised, there is no exact, scientific way to train for something. There is always room for adjustment. Make allowances for rest. Learn the reasons for the training plan and how it might be modified and what ideas alternative plans are based on.

Use a calendar for strategic planning. A calendar lets you develop or keep track of your own training plan. Mark on the calendar the key workouts or training sessions. Mark the final practice (perhaps the final long run). Allow time for a taper before the event to keep you rested and healthy, yet ready. The calendar lets you easily reorganize things in case some life event or sudden awareness of need requires you to change plans. Keep the calendar where you can see it. It will help you whether you are planning a running or strength goal, readying a keynote address, or planning a performance or goal of any kind.

Get involved. Be with like-minded people who are seeking the same thing. A runner will develop better if exposed to other runners. Don't neglect rest.

Add complementary training and activities as needed.

• • •

INTRINSIC ACHIEVEMENT THROUGH COMMITMENT AND PERSISTENCE

Intrinsic achievement is a feeling of gentle joy and self-fulfillment that is the result of internal harmony. It is a lifelong process. Follow through! The words "commitment" and "persistence" echo the process-oriented concept of fitness. There are no quick fixes. Your commitment grows by increasing focus and decreasing conflicting desires according to your pursuit and values. This is commitment without reservation. Nassim Taleb puts it this way: "Many people labor in life under the impression that they are doing something right, yet they may not show solid results for a long time. They need a capacity for adjourned gratification to survive a steady diet of peer cruelty without becoming demoralized. They look like idiots to their cousins, they look like idiots to their peers, they need courage to continue."[104]

Persistence over the long span of time is what carved the Grand Canyon. By the same idea, I cannot lift 2,000 pounds, yet I can easily lift 20 pounds one hundred times, and thus by persisting, I can easily lift 2,000 pounds. Persistence requires us to keep going when there are no obvious signs of immediate reward. Yet persistence forms destiny; it is the mighty force that shapes coastlines, mountains, and continents. Commitment and persistence have a price. It is the sacrifices that come with being willing to persist. As my dad used to say, "You can do anything you want as long as you are willing to pay the price."

· · ·

VALUE PERSISTENCE

You will have setbacks. But they are not failures; they are part of the process. You will bounce back; you will gain resilience. Life's chal-

---

104 Taleb, Nassim Nicholas; *The Black Swan: The Impact of the Highly Improbable, second edition.* Random House Publishing Group, New York; (2010), 87

lenges will come. But you will move on. Humans are ever an odd combination of fragility and invincibility. They are like a branch that can snap off a tree at any moment but also like the mighty oak tree that can stand for one thousand years. Awareness and experience make you aware of your limits, keeping you ever humble. Persistence is the key to long-standing, to a kind of invincibility.

The Latin form of "persist" means "to stand, to be around for a long time, despite obstacles, to remain faithful to a purpose or intent."[105] It is the opposite of the quick fix, the magic bullet, or the super pill or supplement that solves all problems. Expect great results to take time.

Don't look to get it "right" all at once. Forget about right and seek improvement. Getting it right implies no more learning is necessary. Improvement can be continual. Resilience implies bouncing back, not getting it right. Mastery is what you get after thousands of hours of practice with awareness and continual refinement. Mastery itself is relative. Keep going. Persist. Bounce back. As always persistence trumps impatience, and experience outlasts force. No matter how great a start you make, it is nothing without the ability to persist, to see things through to the end.

These ideas will make your training plan real and concrete and lead to many experiences of celebration. As you can see, I have not told you exactly what to do. But I have encouraged self-exploration that leads to a life in which the parts might be integrated into a more harmonious, pleasant, and *fit* life. You are now on the path to great personal fulfillment, your greatest gift to the world

---

105 Harper, Douglas, Historian, persist, Dictionary.com, *Online Etymology Dictionary*, http://www.dictionary.com/browse/persist

CHAPTER 18 LESSON:

COME TO A SITTING POSITION BY ROLLING OVER AN ELBOW SUPPORT

Many gym goers are familiar with the Turkish Get-up. This usually involves holding a weight overhead while lying on your back, then getting up while maintaining the weight's position overhead. This lesson is a modified version of that exercise.

This lesson starts with rising to sitting from a supine (face up) position using an elbow for support because this is a practical movement and one of the many ways we can get up off the floor. You even use elbow support to get out of bed. After mindfully observing how you use your body to raise yourself from these positions, you'll move into an exercise that shows how taking your time while training can result in deeper learning. This is a lesson that applies to areas of life beside exercise.

• • •

Take your time: Allow 30 minutes to complete this lesson.

Part 1: Coming to Sitting by Rolling
over Your Elbow Support

1. Lie on your back with your arms stretched by your sides and your legs stretched out. Take a few moments to notice your contact with the floor. Interlace your hands behind your head and begin to lift it slowly with the help of your elbows. Let your elbows

come together as you lift and apart as you lower your head. Exhale as you lift your head and inhale as you lower your head. Can you feel your abdominal muscles engage as you repeatedly lift and lower your head? Rest your head fully on the ground between each lift, and let your neck muscles completely relax.

2. Unlace your fingers. Rest on your back with your arms at your sides.

3. Tilt your chin toward your chest. Do this several times.

4. Raise your head and look between your legs. Let your arms and hands move downward just a little on the floor in the direction of your feet. Be particularly aware of the action of your abdominal muscles when you raise your head. As you lift your head higher, some of your upper or thoracic vertebrae will come off the floor. When your head is lifted higher, what part of you pushes into the floor?

5. Rest again on your back, and roll your head an inch or two right and left—just enough to relieve any tension in your neck.

6. Raise your head again, but this time lift it with an intention to look at your left foot. Let your ribs roll to the left. Keep your left shoulder and right hand on the floor as your right shoulder rises from the floor and rolls a little to the left.

7. Rest on your back.

8. Slide your left arm out from your body to form a 45-degree angle in relation to your torso.

9. Roll your ribs to the left. Take your more or less straight right arm and reach across to the left side of your body. Your right hand will be in the air reaching toward your left. Allow your head to roll a little to the left. What can your legs do to help the

rolling? How can you coordinate the timing of your reach with the roll of your ribs and the lift of your head?

10. Rest on your back.

11. Again, slide your left arm out to form a 45-degree angle in relation to your torso.

12. Tilt your chin toward your chest, and reach across your body and a little down toward your feet. Keep raising your head, rolling to the left, and reaching with your right hand toward the left until it makes sense to use your left elbow for support and come to a sitting position.

13. Roll back and forth from sitting to lying on your back until it becomes clearer how to use your head, right arm, legs, and elbow support to come to a seated position.

14. Try this on the other side. Do you have clarity and is it, therefore, easy to do on both sides? If it is hard to do on the second side, go back and compare what you are doing on the first side to the second. Rest between each attempt to sit. Is the movement getting easier and clearer?

15. The next time you come to a seated position, you will realize that there are many ways to stand from here.

• • •

Part 2: Rise from the Floor While Holding a Heavy Object

For fun or if you want a challenge, try the following lesson. This is a lesson about incremental training—learning to have patience, practice discipline, and develop deeper interactions with the learning process. You can use this lesson as a concrete example of how to train. If you take your time and are able to generalize the learning you do in this lesson, you will be able to apply the process to many situations in your life.

By engaging with this activity slowly over a five-day period, you will learn to follow a process by stretching out a movement most people would hurry through in one day and to form and follow a clear intention. In sport, this means you know what skill you are practicing. When creating art, you might have an image, a feeling, or a message to convey. When writing, you might start with an outline or a clear notion of the essence of your story or thesis. Having clear intent—or forming a clear intention—means you know what you want to create. You learn to follow through and to learn more thoroughly than when you engage in hurried learning. You practice the kind of learning that is truly yours; you know your subject from all sides.

Doing this causes you to use your imagination to begin a process of discovery and refine your skill so you can experience the idea of repetition without actual repetition because each trial movement is a different movement, a different exploration. Do you see how this training applies to life? Even mathematics is basically one exploration after another built on understanding the essence of what you are working toward.

The goal is to learn and train incrementally. Each time you add resistance to this movement, everything changes. The movement becomes a new movement, and you will need more skill. To learn incrementally is to engage in cycles of learning.

Take your time: Allow five days to complete all the parts in this lesson. Allow 15–30 minutes each day.

• • •

Figure 18.2   *Figure 18.3*

Figure 18.4   *Figure 18.5*

Figure 18.6   *Figure 18.7*

Figure 18.8

Figure 18.9

Day 1

Look at Figures 18.2 to 18.9. Establish the sequence of movements in your mind.

The sequence is this:

- Figure 18.2. Lie on your back with a light object grasped over your right shoulder. (This movement is illustrated with a 5-pound sleeping bag, but you may place your right hand somewhere on your right chest if you don't have access to an appropriately weighted and sized object.)

- Figure 18.2 and 18.3. This time your right arm cannot reach to the right, and your left elbow is placed at a 90-degree angle to your trunk with your palm facing down.

- Figure 18.4. Come to a sitting position over your left elbow.

- Figures 18.5 and 18.6. Come to a sitting position with your left elbow straight by positioning your right leg and left arm in a way that gives good support to your pelvis as you raise it.

- Figure 18.7. Draw your left leg under your body.

- Figure 18.8. Come to a kneeling position on your left knee. Both hands should be off the floor.

- Figure 18.9. Stand.

After you familiarize yourself with the sequence, do the following:

1. Lie on your back without the aid of the illustrations, and imagine coming to sitting by using the support of your left elbow. Imagine the entire sequence all the way to standing. Can you imagine the transition points, the points where you might want to move your hand support or the places where the placement of your hand is important? Can you imagine how this movement

is different from the movements you did in the lesson about coming to standing by rolling over an elbow support because you cannot in this configuration sweep your right hand and arm to the left to help you roll over your left arm? Can you imagine how your right leg might be called upon to help more?

2. After you imagine coming to standing, see if you can imagine reversing the movement with good control through the entire range all the way back to lying on your back. Imagine the entire sequence of movements on the other side with your right hand at a 90-degree angle to your torso, palms down, left knee bent, and with the sole of your foot on the ground.

3. Reverse the movements on the right side in your imagination. Take at least 10–15 minutes to visualize the entire process.

Day 2

1. Lie on your back with your left arm at a 45-degree angle to your torso. Sweep your right arm over to the left like you did in part 1 of this lesson. Now you will do the movement differently; your right hand will be constrained to your right chest and shoulder.

2. Place your right arm on the right side of your chest or hold onto a light object such as a sleeping bag. Now that your right arm cannot sweep to the left to help you come to a sitting position with the left elbow support, how will this movement be different than in the previous lesson?

3. Experiment with the position of your left arm in relation to your torso by moving your left arm closer to your torso and then farther away. Finally, try sitting with left elbow support as you place your left arm at a 90-degree angle in relation to your

torso. What arm position works best? Your head and opposite arm still travel in a path over your left arm support. Can you find the path that makes the best use of your shoulder and right leg to assist as you come to a seated position? If you need to (when bearing a heavy, awkward weight on your right shoulder, for example), use your straight left leg for balance and assistance when you sit over your elbow.

4. Rest and then do this movement with your right arm extended at a 90-degree angle in relation to your torso, and use your left arm to hold onto a sleeping bag or weight. Is the movement as easy to do on this side? If not or if you are not sure, go back to rising over your left elbow. Did you learn anything from doing the movement on one side that you can apply to the other?

5. Rest.

6. Repeat the movement of rising on one elbow to sit, but this time alternate between positioning yourself to rise over your right elbow and then organizing yourself to come to sitting over your left elbow. You come all the way to sitting and then alternate to sit on the other side. Is the movement getting smoother?

7. Rest between sets of repetitions. Rest your head all the way down between each movement. Can you reverse the movement by going from sitting to lying just as smoothly as you come up?

8. Rest and then do a few movements of coming up onto your left elbow and then straightening your left arm to come to an upright sitting position.

9. Do a few movements like this on the right side.

Day 3

1. Lie on your back and visualize coming to a sitting position on your left side and then on your right side. Pretend the weight or sleeping bag on your shoulder weighs 100 pounds. Could you lower it slowly and smoothly back to the ground? How would you do that?

2. Now slide your left arm out on the ground at a 90-degree angle to your torso, and come to sitting over your left elbow support. Did you feel the ground supporting you and lifting you away from the earth?

3. Extend your left arm and come to a full sitting position.

4. Now find support through your right leg and left arm so that you can raise your pelvis and turn your left leg underneath as in Figures 18.4 though 18.7. Then you will need to turn your left knee/leg to come to a position of kneeling on your left knee. You may do this in a separate movement with the support of your right leg and left hand. The placement of your left hand is important. When you are in the sitting position, it is possible to sweep your left hand toward the outside of your left knee. Doing this allows your hand to support the action of pivoting and raising your left knee/leg (see Figures 18.6 and 18.7). Now you are in a position from which you can stand.

Day 4

1. Start in the position shown in Figure 18.7.

2. Come to the standing position by bringing weight over your right leg. At the same time, straighten your left leg. You should feel both legs cooperating to bring you to a standing position.

3. Look at Figure 18.7. Kneel on your left knee, and bend your right knee at a 90-degree angle with your right foot on the floor. Can you reverse the movement of standing with smoothness and good balance at every point? Do you wobble on the way down?

4. Start in the Figure 18.7 position again. As you rise, take note of where your left hand is and when it leaves the ground. Begin to rise and then go back to kneeling. Is it clear to you where you need to put your hand?

5. Stand all the way up again, then kneel. Were you more aware of how to do it and where to put your hand?

6. Stand again, and rest in a standing position.

7. Do the same explorations on the other side, then alternate, getting up once on the left and once on the right.

8. Begin to descend from standing and then change your mind. Instead of descending all the way, go halfway. You are working on the top part of reversing this movement. Change to the other side with the weight or sleeping bag on your other shoulder, and begin to descend and then change your mind, and stand back up.

9. Stop and rest in a standing position.

10. Descend all the way back to the position shown in Figure 18.7, first on one side and then on the other. If you go very, very, slowly, what can you learn about your balance?

Day 5

1. Again, lie on your back as on Day 1. Visualize the entire sequence of movements that you have been doing this week. What is different from the first time you visualized the move-

ments? You have a lot of experience now. Are the movements easier to visualize? Are they clearer? Do you know some critical points to be aware of?

2. Now go from lying on your back to standing in one series of movements. Are there some places where you proceed more smoothly than others? Maybe one side is clearer than the other.

3. Visualize the process once again. Do a few more repetitions of the movement and then rest in any position you would like. You are beginning to master this movement.

4. When you do the movement again, see if it is clear and easy. If it is, perform a few smooth, quick, fluid repetitions of the movement. If you then add weight or do another version, you will enter into this learning cycle again. The point is to give yourself time to learn at your own pace.

. . .

You might not do these exact movements every day, but you may do variations of them (when getting out of bed, for example). This exercise is important, however, because it provides a concrete example of how you might train and how you might succeed by giving yourself ample time to learn. By doing this lesson slowly and over the course of five days, you no doubt learned this movement better than if you had hurried through it. You sensed the details of each step. You felt the differences in each variation. You deepened your ability to perceive. You experimented, and you took time to learn.

CHAPTER 19

Being Fit:
High Intrinsic Achievement

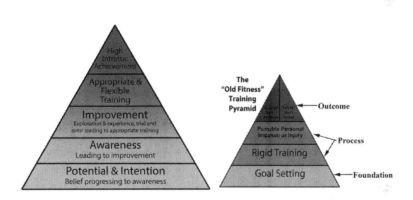

Figure 19.1. Contrasting peaks

It is time to contrast the peaks or final stages of the Old and New Fitness Pyramids. The pinnacle of the New Fitness Pyramid does not represent something separate from the rest of the pyramid, even though I'm discussing it separately here. The top of the pyramid is really a summary of the benefits of being process oriented. The pinnacle is both what the pyramid is all about and an integral part and driver of the process. Intrinsic achievement is the highest reward for being fit. It is what allows you to experience life fully and contribute to others. "Intrinsic" in this context means inherent within you while "extrinsic" means imposed upon you from the outside. Joseph Campbell, in *The Power of Myth*, says, "We're so engaged in doing things to achieve purposes of outer value that we forget the inner value, the rapture that is associated with being alive, is what it is all about."[106]

NEW FITNESS PYRAMID | OLD FITNESS PYRAMID
Figure 19.2 | *Figure 19.3*

- Inward and personal motivation
- Achieving your own dreams
- Potential unlocked
- Personally responsible—"I am the one moving this way"
- Being more than equal to a challenge
- An ongoing process
- Joy in living

- External motivation
- Imposed on you from outside
- Some "thing" possibly accomplished
- Blaming others, your body, genes, coaches, society, the economy
- Being a victim of circumstances
- A temporary result. Not quite satisfied

• • •

106 Flowers, Betty Sue, Editor. Joseph Campbell with Bill Moyer's, *The Power of Myth*, Anchor Books. (1991)

LOFTY INTRINSIC ACHIEVEMENT: MAKING THE IMPOSSIBLE POSSIBLE

In 1993 Stephanie McDuffie Freeman, then a fourteen-year-old, woke up in the hospital and discovered that she had been in a coma for two months and had been given little chance to survive. She had been in an automobile accident, and her life had changed overnight. She was found at the scene nearly dead. Stephanie thought that she would just get up and walk out of the hospital, and that is just what she tried to do. She got out of the wheelchair and fell flat on her face. Nurses and hospital personnel, alarmed, came running to help. It was a humiliating moment but one that defined her. Lying on that hospital floor, feeling embarrassed and hurt, she resolved that no matter what happened, she would find the strength to overcome. This resolve has never left her.

As a result of the injury, her brain had been damaged in areas that were used to control her ability to walk. She knew how to walk, but she couldn't do it. The doctors told her she'd never walk again. But at the time, doctors did not understand how resilient the human brain can be, and her doctors didn't understand the resolve of the person they were talking to. Stephanie wanted to walk; she wanted the life of a normal fourteen-year-old girl. She lay awake at night praying and crying and asking to walk again.

She was in physical therapy for over a year, and during that time she could not attend school. Stephanie was homeschooled and worked diligently to graduate with her class. She learned not only to walk again but also to run. Over time, she was able to run a marathon. To date, she has run six, one of them being the Boston Marathon. The Boston Marathon is unique in that runners must qualify to run it, and the qualifying standards are not easy to meet.

Today Stephanie trains regularly in the gym. She is an aspiring model, writer, trainer, avid runner, and has started a nonprofit organization called Share Your Strong to help others who have traumatic brain injuries.

Stephanie's recovery has been ongoing for the last twenty-four years. She has had to, and readily does, embrace the idea that the journey is more important than the goal. And what is the value of this experience to her? She purchased a 26.2 necklace when she was trying to qualify for the Boston Marathon, and she has not taken it off since. The necklace means the world to her, and because she was told she would never walk again and then ran 26.2 miles, she feels that wearing it signifies what is important and what she is thankful for about her experience. She says that running has given her great joy in life.

This experience has changed her. For many years she identified with that fourteen-year-old girl who struggled so much. But recently, while praying and embracing all her experiences, she had a vision of herself holding the hand of that girl. Fitness is adaptive behavior, and Stephanie's will to overcome and adapt has made her the one extending a helping hand, not just the forlorn child who needs help.

She has found peace, happiness, and strength instead of anxiety and fear. She likes to quote the Dalai Lama: "Happiness is not something ready-made. It comes from your own actions." She greats each new day with gratitude. She has come full circle, and now, after getting a second chance at life, her biggest fear is dying without giving hope and inspiration to others.

• • •

You Are Human

How life came about, no one knows
It's a mystery too deep to plumb
But it did and it grew
Until it was you.
You did nothing to help, yet here you are,
Observing cycles and seasons
That nothing accounts for
It is a certain magic to see the leaves appear on a winter dead tree.
Magic means effective and yet complex
With elements that cannot be seen or touched,
Yet they happen without our help or knowing,
A dependable landmark of life.
And you go through winter and you experience fear
But you dip into a very deep well,
A bottomless shaft inexhaustible
Sensing, feeling, experimenting
And there you find talent, gift and genius.
And you who arose from epochal force and unseen aim
Now avail yourself of the same power,
The power to be human,
The will to do and…
The power of the abstract mind, to order and
change the arrangement of things,
The power to draw on your own intuition,
To know what is lacking, to do what you want,
To use the whole of your body/brain,
To discern the answer and find your way.
It may be that society has covered the mouth of this well

But when you remove the obstructions and look deep down in
You will find what was always there and then
You who were created will also create,
Moment by moment with choice and attention.
The power of the Sun itself
Is now yours
Raise your hands high above your head and shout,
metaphorically or actually as you please,
I I I I I I ... Have Made FIRE!!!
Dare to believe in yourself. Learn, go forth,
Have fun, enjoy, contribute!

• • •

Speaking of fire, Stephanie Freeman says a fire burned in the fourteen-year-old girl she was when she suffered the terrible accident. Than fire, that desire to be strong and fit, has never gone out. For her, fitness is not a burden. It is a deep love. She has never forgotten. And now she uses that fire to ignite her passion for helping others overcome obstacles, train their minds, learn how the brain heals, and be strong.[107]

• • •

A FINAL WORD

There was a young man from our people named Lone Cougar who, when the time came for him to do so, went out to seek a vision. Lone

---

107 All references to Stephanie Freeman are from her blog or from Facebook interviews and appear in this book by permission of Stephanie Freeman.

Cougar went into the mountains alone one day. It was the first time he had been in the wilderness by himself. For four days, he traveled through the mountains, tiring each day, facing his fears, learning to navigate by moon and sun. Five days. Six. His circle brought him back to the plateau above our people's camp. There he sat, hungry, tired, alone, and empty. His hunger for a vision was greater than when he had started his journey. He had a sense of despair. He had no choice. He could not stay out forever. He returned to the village. The wilderness had entered Lone Cougar. He had returned to us somewhat different. The strengths and rhythms of nature pressed into his being. Lone Cougar carried this awareness with him, this new presence, yet all he could focus on was his lack of a vision. Lone Cougar could not help himself. He expressed his disappointment to the old men in the village. They listened to his story knowingly.

They said, "Lone Cougar, you must understand that there are many visions in a lifetime, not only one. You have been strengthened by your experience. The wilderness is more than a place. It is not only without; it is within. And you have indeed received a great vision, for your hunger has increased, and the greater the hunger the greater the purpose. It is your hunger that sustains what you seek. Our people travel often. Someday we will come to a particular place. There will come a particular time. That place and time will define Lone Cougar."

Lone Cougar was drawn back into the wilderness many more times. It was becoming more and more of a home to him, a place he knew and understood. Now he respected the wilderness rather than fearing it. It was becoming an end unto itself, working its lessons ever deeper into him until, at last, Lone Cougar was one with the wilderness. He had been farther than anyone else.

Then one season, the winter was colder. The animals died in great-er numbers. Other people crowded our hunting lands. The summer was hotter with more fires. The creeks ran dry. The animals fled. And then it was Lone Cougar who knew what to do because he had greater knowledge of the surrounding land than the rest of us. It was not strange for Lone Cougar to lead our people. It was the knowledge that was innate within him that he now shared with all. Lone Cougar led our people to better hunting ground than we had before the bad seasons. There we lived and prospered for many, many years. But Lone Cougar had not changed. He continued to expand his knowledge of the land far around him.

In his life, Lone Cougar had many sons and daughters. They learned some of what Lone Cougar had learned but, in time, sought their own visions. Lone Cougar continued along his path to the end of his days. He had learned that life has many paths and that life is one with time and place and that with time and place come destiny.[108]

I hope you take several things from the story of Lone Cougar. True fitness is a process of adaptation and exploration that develops what is innate within us, allows us to live our dreams, and brings self-fulfillment. True fitness in this narrative (and in historical, scientific, and the modern context) is more than exercise or physical fitness. It is a mind-body activity and always involves movement in both thought and body. Movement is the grand tool of self-exploration. True fitness is being able to more than meet the demands of the situation. It is mastering the topography of life. We all have an in-

---

108 Forrester, Scott; *Mysterious Destiny*, Earth Lodge Publishing, Oregon; copyright 2010.

dividual path of self-exploration to take, and self-exploration is the most important form of education. Fitness is a lifelong process. Your personal discoveries equip you for life. And, as you can see from the story of Lone Cougar, this personal knowledge—as it works deeply into you through experience and lifelong purpose—*automatically* enables you to contribute to others, to communicate what you have learned, to improve society. In fact, developing your own voice is the most important thing you can do in life. It is the most important thing you can do for yourself and for others.

There were many examples given in this book of people who overcame their circumstances and adapted to their particular environments. They became fit and so can you. Just as Stephanie Freeman naturally progressed through the trials and experience that led her to found a nonprofit organization and help others, so will your experiences and innate knowledge enable to you to do similar important things.

What Joseph Campbell says is also true: "What each must seek in his life never was on land or sea. It is something out of his own unique potentiality for experience, something that has never been and never could have been experienced by anyone else."[109] That is what we have to gain.

In this chapter, we've reached the pinnacle of the New Fitness Pyramid. Remember that our traditional, culturally accepted definition of fitness is that of physical fitness, yet the actual definition of fitness encompasses self-improvement and self-satisfaction. While those who exercise are concerned with productivity and perhaps muscle size, those who seek real fitness are concerned with enlarging

---

109 https://www.brainyquote.com/quotes/quotes/j/josephcamp160484.html, accessed October 14, 2017.

the whole self, with self-expansion in a more complex way. While exercise may be divorced from awareness and is sometimes called mindless exercise instead of mindful movement, true fitness is about connecting with others, the environment, and ourselves and our purpose on a deeper level. You really are capable of much more than you think if you go deeper, focus, use and commit more of yourself to the task at hand.

Remember too that the Old Fitness Pyramid is where you live much of your life. But the New Fitness Pyramid is for those times when you want to be more than average, when you want to access more of your inherent potential. You can apply the New Fitness Pyramid to all areas of your life. "Life is a process; improve the quality of the process, and you improve the quality of life itself."[110]

And in the end, you will be an Aware Athlete when you learn what *you* need to learn to do what you want, and do it in spite of—and through all—life's circumstances. When you do this, you will live your deepest, most personal dreams.

---

110 Feldenkrais, Moshe, Beringer, Elizabeth, Editor, *Embodied Wisdom, The Collected Papers of Moshe Feldenkrais*, North Atlantic Books, Berkley, CA (2010) Introduction.

CHAPTER 19 LESSON:

THE INTEGUMENTARY LESSON

The integumentary system—your skin— is the largest human organ and covers your whole body. In this lesson, you'll literally and metaphorically explore its boundaries. Literally in that your skin protects the treasure that is your life and metaphorically in that it represents your deepest self and connects you to the world around you. Some caves are legendary because they are said to contain hidden treasure, gold and silver: Your envelope protects the treasure that is your life from the outside environment. Caves have, throughout the ages, symbolized and served as homes and shelters protecting various life forms from the outside environment, and a cave may have a different environment on the inside than on the outside.

Your skin is no different. It helps moderate your body temperature, and your skin (unless you have some kind of cut) protects you from viruses, bacteria, and disease. What a wonderful shelter it is. Your envelope is, on a deeper level, what makes you an individual. Think of the saying "comfortable in your skin." Your skin is precious. You cannot live without it. If too much of your skin is damaged, you'll die.

All of us have commonalities; each are human beings. But if you look closely, you'll find that our anatomies are distinct. Even muscles' origins and insertions are not precisely the same in each person. The structure and shape of our bones are different. Many things are different, yet we all have an envelope. That envelope—our skin—covers our appendages. Our skin covers bone and muscle;

this is a way for us to move and express ourselves in our environments. We are protected from the environment, but not completely isolated.

Now consider that you are 80 percent water. Think about how your skin protects all those hidden fluids that travel in fine tubes throughout your body: tubes and chambers, tubes leading to chambers. The pulmonary system is a system of finer and finer tubes that take in air and move it to the lungs. The digestive system is a system of tubes. The system that circulates blood in your body is a system of finer and finer tubes branching out and carrying fluids and oxygen—life-giving fluids—throughout the body in a way that's very similar to what we see in nature. River systems with tributaries that branch into ever smaller streams are an efficient system for moving water. The tubes within our bodies move oxygen and fluid in much the same way.

In this lesson—done mainly in your imagination—you'll form a deeper connection to your envelope and its contents and develop a new understanding of how you are apart from your environment and a part of it.

· · ·

Take your time: Allow 30 minutes to complete this lesson.

1. Take a few minutes to walk around. Sense the weight of your body on your feet. Sense your height, your width, and your breadth. What is your general sense of self? Where are your thoughts drawn as you do this? What's the quality of your walking? Take a few minutes to sense and explore.

2. Now, find a place to lie down comfortably on the floor. Notice how you feel now. What's the manner in which you are lying? What is your general impression of where your body is making contact with the floor? What are you thinking about?

3. Imagine your envelope: your shape, your skin, your integumentary system. Start with your head. See what you can feel about the shape of yourself. You feel that you have an envelope, a skin, a shape that makes you an individual and separates you from the environment. Visualize the shape of your torso, of your arms, the folds of the skin where you bend. Pause. Continue to explore your envelope. Sense the uniqueness of your enclosure, its one-of-a-kind shape.

4. Mentally observe yourself from head to toe. Picture yourself as a shape formed by skin, a shell. Your shell forms a barrier, a boundary between the outside environment and the inside that contains the essence of you. The shell, the envelope, covers an inside that is hollow. It is hollow yet full of organs and systems that define you. You might say that your envelope encloses you much like a cave.

Many people think of a cave as a chamber within rock. In reality, there are many caves that are much more than holes in rocks. They are, in fact, cave systems. They are composed of corridors (tubes) that lead to chambers and more corridors that run horizontally and vertically. Some cave networks are complicated systems that run for miles below the earth. So, if you picture your skin as a covering for a cave, you would accurately consider yourself a cave system, not a simple cavity. Where we live in Oregon, there is a hollow lava tube a mile long. People walk into this tube and explore its interior. The hollow tube was carved by hot, flowing magma. It originated as a tube, a warm environment, something formed by the hot insides of the planet.

You are, in fact, a hollow tube, a hollow tube with appendages, and those appendages are hollow tubes. As you think about the inside of that hollow tube system, can you sense, feel, or visualize what's inside? Can you sense the fact you are warmer inside than the temperature in the room? Can you feel some division between the outside environment and what's inside of you?

Your skin is your shelter and shield, yet no individual is complete or viable without the special perforations that unite us with the outer environment. We are first of all protected; only then can we be connected.

5. Imagine or sense the texture of your skin. Start at the top of your head, and move down toward your feet.

6. Bring your attention back to your head. Your head has openings: a mouth, nostrils, eyes, ears. You don't simply have an envelope that separates you from your environment. Your eyes bring in light. Explore the texture of your skin, and come to your eyes. Can you feel the light entering through your eyes and the light's energy permeating your tissues?

Your nose, your ears, your vestibular sense in your head all bring you into contact with your environment. What do you hear right now? What do you smell? How does your mouth work to bring nourishment to your body? Can you feel your throat, which houses your vocal cords? Can you feel the potential to make sound even when you are not speaking?

7. Get a general sense of this treasure, this life, this individuality that's housed within your envelope. Think of your breath and

how it brings in life, energy. Can you feel the oxygen entering your lungs? Can you imagine it energizing your tissues? Can you imagine your envelope protecting your uniqueness?

8. Slowly roll over and get up. Come to your feet. Feel your weight on your feet. Remember how you felt when you started this lesson?

9. Shift your attention back to the treasure that's contained within your envelope, your skin, yourself. Walk around. Do you notice—sense—anything different in your walk and how you feel on your feet? Take several minutes to explore how your body moves when you walk. Notice where your thoughts are drawn.

Your envelope, on a deeper level, is what makes you an individual. You must have some distinction between you and the outside world, something that makes you you—an individuum.[111] What will you do with the treasure contained within your skin?

What is your potential?

---

111 individuum. Mirriam-Webster dictionary online. Accessed 11/12/2017. https://www.merriam-webster.com/dictionary/individuum

READING LIST

Awareness Through Movement: Easy-to-Do Health Exercises to Improve Your Posture, Vision, Imagination, and Personal Awareness, Feldenkrais, Moshe; Harper Collins Publisher, New York; copyright 1972

Focusing; Gendlin, Eugene T. PhD; Bantum Books, New York, New York; copyright 1978

Focus: The Hidden Driver of Excellence, Goleman, Daniel; Bloomsberry, New York; copyright 1978

How Champions Think: In Sports and in Life; Rotella, Robert; Simon and Schuster, New York, New York; copyright 2015

Intelligence in the Flesh: Why Your Mind Needs Your Body Much More than You Think Intelligence in the Flesh; Claxton, Guy; Yale University Press, New Haven, Connecticut; copyright 2015

Into the Magic Shop: A Neurosurgeon's Quest to Discover the Mysteries of the Brain and the Secrets of the Heart; Doty, James R. MD; Penguin Random House LLC, New York, New York; copyright 2016

Man's Search for Meaning; the Classic Tribute to Hope from the Holocaust; Frankl, Viktor E.; Beacon Press, Boston, Massachusetts; copyright 1959

Mindset: The New Psychology of Success; Dweck, Carol S, PhD., Ballentine Books, New York, New York; copyright 2016

Moshe Feldenkrais: A Life in Movement; Reese, Mark; Reese Kress Somatic Press, San Rafael, CA; copyright 2015.

The Brain That Changes Itself: Stories of Personal Triumph from the Frontiers of Brain Science; Doidge, Norman; Penguin Books, New York, New York; copyright 2007

The Brain's Way of Healing: Remarkable Discoveries and Recoveries from the Frontiers of Neuroplasticity; Doidge, Norman; Penguin Books, New York, New York; copyright

The Craft of the Warrior; Spencer, Robert; Frog Books, Berkley, California; copyright 1993

The Elusive Obvious or Basic Feldenkrais; Feldenkrais, Moshe; Meta Publications, Soquel, California; copyright 1981

The Mass Psychology of Fittism: Fitness, Evolution and the First Two Laws of Thermodynamics; Yu, Edward; Independent Publisher; copyright 2005

The Mind and the Brain: Neuroplasticity and the Power of Mental Force; Schwartz, Jeffrey M. and Begley, Sharon; HarperCollins, New York, New York; copyright 2002

The Mindful Athlete: Secrets of Pure Performance, Mumford George; Parallax Press, Berkley, California; copyright 2015

The Potent Self; Feldenkrais, Moshe; Frog LTD and Somatic Resources, Berkley, California; copyright 1985

The Power of Habit: Why We Do What We Do in Life and Business; Duhigg, Charles; Random House, New York, New York; copyright 2012

The Power of Myth; Campbell, Joseph with Moyers, Bill, and Flowers, Betty Sue, Editor; Anchor Books, New York, New York; copyright 1991

The Thinking Body: Study of the Balancing Forces of Dynamic Man; Todd, Mable Ellsworth and Bracket, E. G.; Gestalt Journal Press, Gouldsboro, Maine; copyright 1937, 2008

The Upside of Stress: Why Stress Is Good and How We Get Good at It; McGonigal, Kelly; Penguin Random House, 375 Hudson Street, New York, New York 10014, copyright 2016

BIBLIOGRAPHY

adventure. Dictionary.com. *Collins English Dictionary - Complete & Unabridged 10th Edition.* HarperCollins Publishers. http://www.dictionary.com/browse/adventure?s=t

Allen, James, written in contemporary language by Charles Conrad. *As a Man Thinketh, 21st Century Edition.* Best Success Books. 2017.

athlete. Dictionary.com. *Dictionary.com Unabridged.* Random House, Inc. http://www.dictionary.com/browse/athlete?s=t

Atlas Obscura. "The Last Incan Suspension Bridge Is Made Entirely of Grass and Woven By Hand". Slate. June 10, 2013. http://www.slate.com/blogs/atlas_obscura/2013/06/10/the_last_incan_suspension_bridge_is_made_entirely_of_grass_and_woven_by.html

Attenborough, David. "The Life of Mammals: Food for Thought", BBC. August 2017. Volume 10. http://www.bbc.co.uk/programmes/b007c1vc

Attenborough, David. "Human Mammal, Human Hunter: Life of Mammals". BBC Earth. November 6, 2009. https://www.youtube.com/watch?v=826HMLoiE_o

BBC. "Lessons I've Learned: Steve Backley". BBC Sports. May 8, 2007. http://news.bbc.co.uk/sport2/hi/athletics/skills/6615335.stm

Beilock, Sian, PhD. "How Humans Learn: Lessons from the Sea Squirt". Choke, Psychology Today. July 11, 2012. https://www.psychologytoday.com/blog/choke/201207/how-humans-learn-lessons-the-sea-squirt

Campbell, Joseph. Flowers, Betty Sue, Editor. *Joseph Campbell The Power of Myth with Bill Moyers.* Anchor Books. 1991.

Campbell, Joseph. Joseph Campbell Quotes. BrainyQuote.com. Xplore Inc,. 2017. https://www.brainyquote.com/quotes/quotes/j/josephcamp160484.html

Canfield, Jack and Dr. Peter Chee. *Coaching for Breakthrough Success: Proven Techniques for Making Impossible Dreams Possible.* McGraw Hill Education, New York. 2013. 123.

Carrier, Scott. *Running After Antelope.* Counterpoint, Washington DC. 2001.

Carroll, Pete, with Yogi Roth and Kristoffer A. Garmin. *Win Forever: Live, Work and Play Like a Champion.* Portfolio/Penguin. 2011

Chang, Louise, MD. Reviewed by. "Mind and Body Fitness for Lifelong Good Health". Web, LLC. February 1, 2006. paragraph 2. http://www.webmd.com/fitness-exercise/features/mind-body-fitness-lifelong-good-health#1

Conservation Institute.org. "10 Fastest Animals on Earth, #5 Pronghorn Antelope". Conservation Institute. 2017. http://www.conservationinstitute.org/10-fastest-animals-on-Earth/

Coué, Émile. "My Method". Double Day, Page and Company. 1923. http://www.artleidecker.com/wp-content/uploads/2015/04/Coue_My_Method_12-20-99.pdf

Doidge, Norman. *The Brain That Changes Itself: Stories of Personal Triumph from the Frontiers of Brain Science.* Penguin Books, New York. 2007. 88, 197, 201, 204, 209.

Dunning, David and Justin Kruger. "Unskilled and Unaware of It: How Difficulties in Recognizing One's Own Incompetence Lead to Inflated Self-Assessments". Journal of Personality and Psychology. 1999. Vol 77, No 96, 1121-1134. http://psych.colorado.edu/~vanboven/teaching/p7536_heurbias/p7536_readings/kruger_dunning.pdf

Dweck, Carol S, PhD. *Mindset: The New Psychology of Success.* Ballentine, New York. 2016.

Edison, Thomas. "Innovate Like Edison". National Park Service, Department of the Interior, Washington DC. September 3, 2017. https://www.nps.gov/edis/learn/education/index.htm

Feldenkrais, Moshe. *A Life in Movement*, Reese Kress Somatic Press. San Rafael, CA. 2015. 458.

Feldenkrais, Moshe. *Awareness Through Movement.* Harper Collins Publishers, New York, New York. 1972. 36th point number 7, 36, 38, 40.

Feldenkrais, Moshe. Beringer, Elizabeth, Editor. *Embodied Wisdom; The Collected Papers of Moshe Feldenkrais.* North Atlantic Books, Berkley, CA. 2010. Introduction.

Feldenkrais, Moshe. *Body Awareness as Healing Therapy: The Case of Nora.* Frog Books, Berkley, California. 1993. XIV.

Feldenkrais, Moshe. *Body and Mature Behavior.* Frog LTD and Somatic Resources, 830 Bancroft way, #112 Berkeley California 94710. 1949. 218.

Feldenkrais, Moshe. *The Elusive Obvious.* Meta Publications, 3601 Caldwell Dr. Soquel, CA 95073. 1981.

Feldenkrais, Moshe. Feldenkrais Guild of North America. 2017. https://feldenkrais.com

Feldenkrais Moshe. Lectures Given in Cern, Switzerland. Paul Dorn, October 17, 2014. https://www.youtube.com/watch?v=SBypfdEuDO0 and https://www.youtube.com/watch?v=JaIvaU6XvCM and part 3 https://www.youtube.com/watch?v=ZYuW5hDDw4s and part 4 https://www.youtube.com/watch?v=yNfB0WOnu74

Feldenkrais, Moshe, PhD. "Mind and Body." *Two lectures in Systematics: The Journal of the Institute for the Comparative Study of History, Philosophy and the Sciences*, 1964.Vol. 2, No.1, June. Reprinted in *Your Body Works*, Gerald Kogan (ed.). Berkeley: Transformations, 1980. http://www.feldenkrais-method.com/wp-   content/uploads/2014/11/Mind-and-Body-Moshe-Feldenkrais.pdf

Feldenkrais, Moshe. *The Potent Self*. Frog Books, 830 Bancroft Way #112, Berkley, CA 94710. 1985. foreword xxx.

Feldenkrais, Moshe. Self Discovery for You. 2010-2017. http://www.self-discovery-for-you.com/moshe-feldenkrais.html

Forestiere Historical Center. Wilton, CA. 2006-2007. http://www.forestiere-historicalcenter.com/Forestierebio.html

Forrester, Scott. *Mysterious Destiny*. Earth Lodge Publishing, Oregon. 2010.

Frankl, Viktor E. *Man's Search for Meaning*. Beacon Press, Boston. 1959.

Fritz, Robert. *The Path of Least Resistance: Learning to Become the Creative Force in Your Own Life*. Random House Publishing, New York, New York. 1984.

Gandhi, Mahatma. "Greatest Quotes of Mahatma Gandhi - My Life Is My Message". Heart Fables. March 23, 2015. https://www.youtube.com/watch?v=5jvdhGqvmLo

Gendlin, Eugene, PhD. *Focusing*. Bantam Books. 1978.

Gugliotta, Guy. "The Great Human Migration: Why Humans Left Their African Homeland 80,000 Years Ago to Colonize the World". Smithsonian Magazine. July 2008. http://www.smithsonianmag.com/history/the-great-human-migration-13561/?sessionguid=c4932ea9-a752-1aa9-062e-83999a5738a3&no-ist=&page=1

Hamilton, David R. *It's the Thought That Counts: Why Mind Over Matter Really Works.* Hay House Inc. Introduction and Chapters 1 and 2.

Handel, Steven. "Wisdom of Ignorance: Knowing What You Don't Know". The Emotion Machine. April 6, 2013. http://www.theemotionmachine.com/wisdom-in-ignorance-knowing-what-you-dont-know/

Heinrich, Bernd. *Racing the Antelope: What Animals Can Teach Us About Running and Life.* Harper Collins, New York, New York. 2001.

Henry, Kris. "Fosbury Was No Flop". Mail Tribune. April 24, 2016. http://www.mailtribune.com/special/20160424/fosbury-was-no-flop

Hill, Napoleon. *Think and Grow Rich*. Napoleon Hill Foundation. Wise, Virginia. 1937.

History.com staff. "Inca". History.com, A+E Networks, 2015. http://www.history.com/topics/inca

Lee, Bruce, *Bruce Lee Jeet Kune Do*. Tuttle Publishing, North Clarendon Vermont. 1997. Section 6: Beyond System.

Lewis, C.S. *The Problem of Pain;* Samizdat. University Press, Quebec, Canada. 1940.

Liebenberg, Louis. *The Art of Tracking: The Origin of Science.* David Phillip Publishers, South Africa. 1990.

Lieberman, Daniel E. and Dennis M. Bramble. "The Evolution of Marathon Running: Capabilities in Humans". Sports Medicine 2007. 37(4-5): 288- 290. https://dash.harvard.edu/bitstream/handle/1/3716644/lieberman_marathon.pdf?sequence=3

limitations. Dictionary.com. *Dictionary.com Unabridged.* Random House, Inc. http://www.dictionary.com/browse/limitations

Lopez, Barry. *Arctic Dreams: Imagination and Desire in a Northern Landscape.* Vintage Books, New York. 1986. 278, 291, 202.

Louveau, Antonie and Igor Smirnov, et al. *Structural and Functional Features of Central Nervous System Lymphatic Vessels.* Nature: International Weekly Journal of Science. July 16, 2013. 523, 337-331. doi:10.1038/nature14432 http://www.techtimes.com/articles/58602/20150608/researchers-uncover-missing-link-between--and-immune-system.htm.

magic. Dictionary.com. *Dictionary.com Unabridged.* Random House, Inc. http://www.dictionary.com/browse/magic?s=t

Main, Douglas. "Chimps Have Better Short-Term Memories Than Humans". February 16, 2013. http://www.livescience.com/27199-chimps-smarter-memory-humans.html

McDougall, Christopher. *Born to Run: A Hidden Tribe, Superathletes, and the Greatest Race the World Has Never Seen.* Alfred A. Knopf, New York. 2009.

McGonigal, Kelly, PhD. *The Upside of Stress: Why Stress Is Good for You and How to Get Good at It.* Penguin Random House, 375 Hudson Street, New York, New York 10014. 2015.

McMahon, Kathy. "The Survival Mindset". Resilience. March 2010. Post Carbon Institute, 800 SW Washington Ave.

Suite 5, Corvallis OR97333. http://www.resilience.org/stories/2010-03-15/survival-mindset

Merzenich, Michael, et al. "Brain Plasticity-Based Therapeutics". Human Neuroscience. V8. 2014.

Millman, Dan. *Way of the Peaceful Warrior: A Book that Changes Lives*. H. J. Kramer. 1984.

Mills, Billy. "How to Visualize". One Vision Board. March 21, 2012. https://www.youtube.com/watch?v=Fx1GBrQEzjw

Milroy, Andy. *"North American Ultrarunning: A History"*. JMD Media. 2012.

Mumford, George and Phil Jackson. *The Mindful Athlete: Secrets to Pure Performance*. Parallax Press, Berkeley, California. 2015. 128.

New York Times. "Climbing Mount Everest Is Work for Supermen". The New York Times, March 18, 1923. http://graphics8.nytimes.com/packages/pdf/arts/mallory1923.pdf

persist. Dictionary.com. *Online Etymology Dictionary*. Douglas Harper, Historian. http://www.dictionary.com/browse/persist

plastic. Dictionary.com. *Dictionary.com Unabridged*. Random House, Inc. http://www.dictionary.com/browse/plastic?s=t

Pompei, Dan. "Inside Manning" Sports on Earth. MLB Advanced Media, L.P. 2017. http://www.sportsonEarth.com/article/91281874/to-understand-peyton-manning-one-has-to--where-he-came-from

Port, Michael. *Steal the Show*. Houghton Miffin Harcourt Publishing Company, New York. 2015. 55.

Powell, Hugh, Editor. "Arctic Tern". The Cornell Lab of Ornithology. Cornell University. Ithica, New York. 2015. https://www.allaboutbirds.org/guide/Arctic_Tern/id

Ratey, John J. and Richard Manning. *Go Wild: Free Your Body and Mind from the Afflictions of Civilization*. Little Brown and Co, New York. 2014. 99-100.

The Reader's Digest, Volume 51. (Filler item). The Reader's Digest Association. Quote Page 64. (Verified on paper.) https://quote-investigator.com/2015/02/03/you-can/#note-10545-1

Richardson, Alan. "Mental Practice: A Review and Discussion Part 1". Association For Health, Physical Education And Recreation, Research Quarterly. American Association for Health, Physical Education and Recreation. 1967Vol. 38 Iss.1. http://www.tandfonline.com/doi/pdf/10.1080/10671188.1967.10614808?needAccess=true

Rotella, Bob. *How Champions Think*. Simon and Schuster, New York. 2015. 8.

Schwartz, Jeffrey, MD. and Sharon Begley. *The Mind and the Brain: Neuroplasticity and the Power of Mental Force*. Harper Collins E-books, New York. 2002, 201.

Schwarzenegger, Arnold. "Arnold Schwarzenegger's Keys to Success. Million Dollar Baby Fitness". October 1, 2012. https://www.youtube.com/watch?v=UOUVkISESKc

Secunda, Brant and Mark Allen. *Fit Soul, Fit Body: 9 Keys to a Healthier, Happier You*. Ben Bella Books Inc. Dallas, TX. 2008. 9, 13.

Smithsonian Air and Space Museum. "Man Around the Moon, Apollo 9: AS-503". National Air and Space Museum, Washington, DC. https://airandspace.si.edu/explore-and-learn/topics/apollo/apollo-program/orbital-missions/apollo8.cfm

Sparks, T Austin, *But Ye Are Come unto Mount Zion*. Austin Sparks Net. 1969. Chapter 1. http://www.austin-sparks.net/english/books/003986.html

Starika, Sharon. Sharon's Story. Sharon Starika Movement
    Educator. 2011. http://sharonstarika.com/

Strong, James. *Strong's Exhaustive Concordance of the Bible*
    Hendrickson Publishers. 2007.

Suzuki, Shunryu. *Zen Mind, Beginners Mind.* Weatherhill, New
    York. 1970. https://www.goodreads.com/author/quotes/62707.
    Shunryu_Suzuki

Taleb, Nassim Nicholas. *The Black Swan: The Impact of the Highly
    Improbable, second edition.* Random House Publishing Group,
    New York. 2010. 16, 87.

Taub, E. "Parallels Between Use of Constraint-Induced Movement
    Therapy to Treat Neurological Motor Disorders and
    Amblyopia Training". Developmental. Psychobiology. 2012.
    54: 274–292. doi:10.1002/dev.20514

Todd, Mable Ellsworth; *The Thinking Body: Study of the Balancing
    Forces of Dynamic Man.* Gestalt   Journal Press. Gouldsboro,
    ME. 2008.

Todd, Mabel. *The Thinking Body: Study of the Balancing Forces of
    Man.* Princeton Book Co, Publishers, Hightstown, New Jersey.
    1937. Chapter 1.

transformation. Dictionary.com. *Dictionary.com Unabridged.*
    Random House, Inc. http://www.dictionary.com/browse/
    transformation

Wilkins, Jayne and Benjamin J. Schoville, et al. *An Experimental
    Investigation of the Functional Hypothesis and Evolutionary
    Advantage of Stone-Tipped Spears.* PLoS One. August 27, 2014.
    doi: 10.1371/journal.pone.0104514 https://www.ncbi.nlm.
    nih.gov/pmc/articles/PMC4146534/

Wolkin, Jennifer. "Meet Your Second Brain: The Gut". Mindful. Foundation for a Mindful Society. August 14, 2015. http://www.mindful.org/meet-your-second-brain-the-gut/

Yu, Edward. *The Art of Slowing Down: A Sense-able Approach to Running Faster*. Panenthea, Harrisburg, PA. 2001. 76.

Yu, Edward. *The Mass Psychology of Fittism: Fitness, Evolution and the First Two Laws of Thermodynamics*. Undocumented Worker Press. 2015. 329

INDEX

71361645R00196

Made in the USA
Middletown, DE
22 April 2018